LIFE ESSENTIAL:
THE HOPE OF THE GOSPEL

GEORGE MACDONALD

Life Essential
The Hope of the Gospel

edited by Rolland Hein

Harold Shaw Publishers
Wheaton, Illinois

The Hope of the Gospel was first published in 1892.

Library of Congress Catalog Card Number 74-16732

ISBN 0-87788-499-4

Printed in the United States of America

90 89   5 4

INTRODUCTION
7

1. SALVATION FROM SIN
13

2. THE REMISSION OF SINS
21

3. JESUS IN THE WORLD
28

4. JESUS AND HIS FELLOW TOWNSMEN
33

5. THE HEIRS OF HEAVEN AND EARTH
41

6. SORROW THE PLEDGE OF JOY
49

7. GOD'S FAMILY
55

8. THE REWARD OF OBEDIENCE
63

9. THE YOKE OF JESUS
67

10. THE SALT AND THE LIGHT OF THE WORLD
77

11. THE RIGHT HAND AND THE LEFT
85

12. THE HOPE OF THE UNIVERSE
91

INTRODUCTION

"Life and religion are one, or neither is anything. . . . Religion is no way of life, no show of life, no observance of any sort. . . . It is life essential. . . . The man to whom virtue is but the ornament of character, something over and above, not essential to it, is not yet a man."

Thus George MacDonald concludes in one of his many novels, *The Marquis of Lossie*. The deepest conviction of his life and writings was that life without true religion is no real life at all, and growth in virtue is growth into life itself.

MacDonald's writings have helped many to Christian conversion, one of the most well known being C. S. Lewis. Lewis's conversion was precipitated by his discovery of MacDonald's mythopoeic novel, *Phantastes* (1858), and many of Lewis's ideas may be traced to MacDonald's thought. People who are searching carefully for truth will find in reading MacDonald a strength of Christian vision and an aptness of psychological insight that have a compelling appeal.

He was a prolix writer in a century of prolix writers. Living through the Victorian era, he published over fifty books, and these in impressive variety: novels, fantasies, children's fairy tales, short stories, essays in literary criticism, and sermons. His Christian convictions permeate all of these, but *The Hope of the Gospel,* a volume of theological essays written late in his career (1892), summarizes well his essential ideas. Our volume is a condensation of that work.

MacDonald's convictions must be understood in terms of the forces that shaped them. Born in 1824 in northern Scotland, he lost his mother as a child of eight. His father, a strict yet loving man of strong Calvinist persuasion, became both father and mother to his large family. MacDonald's very close relationship with his father continued until the old man's death in 1858. The grown son's regular correspondence with him reveals how ideal this relationship was. It was in this context that the Biblical image of God as our Heavenly Father spoke so powerfully to MacDonald, and he never tired of exploring its theological implications.

Further, MacDonald came to feel that God could not possibly be less compassionate than such a father, although, unlike any man, God is altogether just. Sitting once at a dinner among his literary friends—MacDonald knew many of the notable writers of his day, such as Thackeray, Dickens, Arnold, and Ruskin—he was fascinated to hear a journalist recite an old Scotch epitaph:

Here lie I, Martin Elginbrodde;
Hae mercy o' my soul, Lord God;
As I wad do, were I Lord God,
An' ye war Martin Elginbrodde!

This verse not only furnished MacDonald with the kernel idea for his first novel (an unpublished one), but it also gave a vivid concrete expression to his deep theological conviction of the nature of God.

Although MacDonald's vision of God's mercy never compromises God's justice, as it does in theologies of liberal persuasion, it nevertheless brought the young Mac-

Donald's thinking into conflict with that of many members of the Scottish religious community. The doctrine that God elects some people to heaven and damns others to hell simply to illustrate His mercy and His holiness respectively, overlooking the moral quality of their lives, was deeply offensive to him. "I well remember feeling as a child that I did not care for God to love me if He did not love everybody: the kind of love I needed was the love that all men needed, the love that belonged to their nature as the children of the Father, a love He could not give me except He gave it to all men," he writes in *Weighed and Wanting*, a later novel. A majority of the members of the Congregational Church at Arundel—which he was pastoring in 1852—did not sympathize with the sweep of his vision, and forced him to resign.

His objectors accused him of being tainted with German theology. While as a student, MacDonald had spent a summer in a castle in the far North of Scotland cataloging a neglected library, and there he did indeed encounter German romanticism. The mystical poetry and the great fairy tales of such writers as Novalis and Hoffman impressed him most. He was fascinated with their vision of the universe of God as one great, harmonious whole, and of man as growing into a fuller realization of this harmony. Man's life on the highest level is a quest for the eternal and the infinite.

MacDonald's theology is, then, a synthesis of these elements of his experience: his relation to his father, his childhood training in the tenets of Scottish Calvinism, and his fascination as a young adult with German romantic idealism. From the first he derived a large sense of the mercy of God; from the second, a deep conviction of God's justice; and from the third, a comprehensive vision of the potential of man for spiritual growth. Life and religion are, indeed, one. All men are potential sons of God and are moving in their spiritual lives either toward or away from becoming sons of God in actual fact. Christian conversion is a turning toward God, enabling the Christian henceforth by the power of God to deal with sins successively in his life and to grow in likeness to God in the quality of his character.

God is filled with love to man, and His spirit is in all of the circumstances of a man's life, reaching out to him and helping him—if he will but respond—to come into full sonship through obedience. MacDonald is bold to desire that all men will become sons of God—in another life if not in this—not because God will take a light view of their sins, but because they may eventually come to perceive both their own selves and the true nature of their sin as God sees them. The love of God is absolutely just; it will have nothing short of final purity in the lives of all with whom He will fellowship. It is as a fire, consuming all that is unlovely in the beloved, and working to perfect their beings in true sonship.

MacDonald is a courageous thinker, and his vision of the destiny of man answers to what is deepest in the heart of all good men. Greville, MacDonald's biographer son, records: "Once one of us said to him: 'It all seems too good to be true!' But he answered: 'Nay, it is just so good it must be true!' "[1]

A careful student of Scripture, MacDonald sought its deeper meanings intensely. "I am always finding out meaning which I did not see before, and which I now cannot see perfectly—for, of course, till my heart is like Christ's great heart, I cannot fully know what He meant" he wrote to his father in 1853, and again, the same year: "O, I know a little now, and only a little, what Christ's deep sayings mean, about becoming like a child, about leaving all for Him, about service, and truth and love. God is our loving, true, self-forgetting friend. All delight, all hope and beauty are in God."[2] Growth in the quality of one's inner being is requisite to spiritual understanding; the more one understands, the more he sees that the loving God who stands at the heart of all things, bringing men to goodness and virtue, is the answer to all the riddles of life.

MacDonald spent his life energetically communicating the meaning of life as he understood it. Although he lectured widely—he toured the United States in 1873—his was chiefly a ministry of writing, and he gave himself to it throughout his long lifetime with amazing stamina and perseverance. Many of his works went through a great number of editions in both England and America, attesting to an immense popularity in his day.

People of his day, however, relished a considerably more verbose and florid style in writing then readers of our own. MacDonald's *The Hope of the Gospel* is one of the very finest devotional volumes I have ever read, but, it suffers from a rambling and repetitious style. My undertaking has been, humbly and cautiously, to reduce these sermons to their more essential statements. In so doing, I have decreased their volume by approximately one half.

These deletions are not indicated by ellipses except when they have occurred within a single sentence. Bible quotations have been changed from the King James Version to the Revised Standard Version.

Rolland Hein
July 1974

---

[1]*George MacDonald and His Wife* (London: George Allen & Unwin Ltd.), p. 172.
[2]*Ibid.*, p.184.

1
SALVATION
FROM SIN

" . . . and you shall call his name Jesus,
for he will save
his people from their sins."
Matthew 1:21.

I would help some to understand what Jesus came from the
home of our Father to be to us and do for us. Everything in
the world is more or less misunderstood at first: we have to
learn what it is, and come at length to see that it must be so,
that it could not be otherwise. Then we know it; and we
never know a thing *really* until we know it thus.

I presume there is scarce a human being who, resolved
to speak openly, would not confess to having something
that plagued him, something from which he would gladly
be free, something rendering it impossible for him, at the
moment, to regard life an altogether good thing. Most men,
I presume, imagine that, free of such things antagonistic,
life would be an unmingled satisfaction, worthy of being
prolonged indefinitely.

The causes of their discomfort are of all kinds, and the
degrees of it reach from simple uneasiness to a misery such
as makes annihilation the highest hope of the sufferer.
Perhaps the greater part of the energy of this world's life

goes forth in the endeavor to rid itself of discomfort.

However absurd the statement may appear to one who has not yet discovered the fact for himself, the cause of every man's discomfort is evil, moral evil—first of all, evil in himself, his own sin, his own wrongness, his own un-rightness; and then, evil in those he loves: with this latter I have not now to deal; the only way to get rid of it is for the man to get rid of his own sin. No special sin may be recognizable as having caused this or that special physical discomfort—which may indeed have originated with some ancestor—but evil in ourselves is the cause of its continuance, the source of its necessity.

The evil is *essentially* unnecessary, and passes with the attainment of the object for which it is permitted—namely the development of pure will in many. The suffering also is essentially unnecessary, but while the evil lasts, the suffering, whether consequent or merely concomitant, is absolutely necessary.

The Cure

Foolish is the man, and there are many such men, who would rid himself or his fellows of discomfort by setting the world right, by waging war on the evils around him, while he neglects that integral part of the world where lies his business, his first business—namely, his own character and conduct.

There is no way of making three men right but by making right each one of the three; but a cure in one man who repents and turns is a beginning of the cure of the whole human race.

Rightness alone is cure. The return of the organism to its true self is its only possible ease. To free a man from suffering, he must be set right, put in health; and the health at the root of man's being, his rightness, is to be free from wrongness, that is, from sin. A man is right when there is no wrong in him. The wrong, the evil is in him; he must be set free from it.

The Lord never came to deliver men from the consequences of their sins while yet those sins remained: that
would be to cast out of the window the medicine of cure
while yet the man lay sick; to go dead against the very laws
of being. Yet men, loving their sins, and feeling nothing of
their dread hatefulness, have, consistent with their low
condition, constantly taken this word concerning the Lord
[Matt. 1:21] to mean that He came to save them from the
punishment of their sins. This idea—this miserable fancy,
rather—has terribly corrupted the preaching of the gospel.
The message of the good news has not been truly delivered.

The mission of Jesus was from the same source and with
the same object as the punishment of our sins. He came to
work along with our punishment. He came to side with it,
and set us free from our sins. No man is safe from hell until
he is free from his sins; free of them, hell itself would be
endurable to him.

For hell is God's and not the devil's. Hell is on the side of
God and man, to free the child of God from the corruption
of death. Not one soul will ever be redeemed from hell but
by being saved from his sins, from the evil in him. If hell be
needful to save him, hell will blaze, and the worm will
writhe and bite, until he takes refuge in the will of the
Father.

Salvation from Live Sins

"Salvation from hell" is salvation as conceived by such
to whom hell and not evil is the terror. But if even for
dread of hell a poor soul seek the Father, he will be heard
of Him in his terror, and, taught of Him to seek the immeasurably greater gift, will in the greater receive the less.

There is another important misapprehension of the
words of the messengers of the good tidings—that they
threaten us with punishment because of the sins we have
committed; whereas, their message is of forgiveness, not of
vengeance; of deliverance, not of evil to come. Not for anything he has committed do they threaten a man with the

outer darkness. Not for any or all of his sins that are past shall a man be condemned; not for the worst of them needs he dread remaining unforgiven. The sin he dwells in, the sin he will not come out of, is the sole ruin of a man.

His present, his live sins—those pervading his thoughts and ruling his conduct; the sins he keeps doing, and will not give up; the sins he is called to abandon, and clings to; the same sins which are the cause of his misery, though he may not know it—these are they for which he is even now condemned. "This is the judgment, that the light has come into the world, and men loved darkness rather than light, because their deeds were evil."

It is the indwelling badness, ready to produce bad actions, that we need to be delivered from. Against this badness if a man will not strive, he is left to commit evil and reap the consequences. To be saved from these consequences would be no deliverance; it would be an immediate, ever deepening damnation. It is the evil in our being —no essential part of it, thank God—the miserable fact that the very child of God does not care for his Father and will not obey Him, causing us to desire wrongly, act wrongly, or, where we try not to act wrongly, yet making it impossible for us not to feel wrongly—this is what He came to deliver us from—not the things we have done, but the possibility of doing such things any more.

With the departure of this possibility, and with the hope of confession hereafter to those we have wronged, will depart also the power over us of the evil things we have done, and so we shall be saved from them also. The bad that lives in us, our evil judgments, our unjust desires, our hate and pride and envy and greed and self-satisfaction—these are the souls of our sins, our live sins, more terrible than the bodies of our sins, namely, the deeds we do, inasmuch as they not only produce these loathsome things, but make us loathsome as they.

Our wrong deeds are our dead works; our evil thoughts are our live sins. These, the essential opposites of faith and love, the sins that dwell and work in us, are the sins from which Jesus came to deliver us. When we turn against them and refuse to obey them, they rise in fierce insistence, but the same moment begin to die. We are then on the Lord's side, as He has always been on ours, and He begins to deliver us from them.

As the love of Him who is love transcends ours as the heavens are higher than the earth, so must He desire in His child infinitely more than the most jealous love of the best mother can desire in hers. He would have him rid of all discontent, all fear, all grudging, all bitterness in word or thought, all gauging and measuring of his own with a different rod from that he would apply to another's. He will have no curling of the lip; no indifference in him to the man whose service in any form he uses; no desire to excel another, no contentment at gaining by his loss. He will not have him receive the smallest service without gratitude; would not hear from him a tone to jar the heart of another, a word to make it ache, be the ache ever so transient. From such, as from all other sins, Jesus was born to deliver us; not, primarily, or by itself, from the punishment of any of them. When all are gone, the holy punishment will have departed also. He came to make us good, and therein blessed children.

Willing His Will

One master-sin is at the root of all the rest. It is the absence in the man of harmony with the Being whose thought is the man's existence, whose word is the man's power of thought. For the highest creation of God in man is his will, and until the highest in man meets the highest in God, their true relation is not yet a spiritual fact.

The relation exists, but while one of the parties neither knows, loves, nor acts upon it, the relation is, as it were, yet unborn. The highest in man is neither his intellect nor his imagination nor his reason; all are inferior to his will, and indeed, in a grand way, dependent upon it: his will must meet God's—a will *distinct* from God's, else were no *harmony* possible between them.

Not the less, therefore, but the more, is all God's. For God creates in the man the power to will His will. It may cost God a suffering man can never know, to bring the man to the point at which he will will His will; but when he is brought to that point, and declares for the truth—that is, for the will of God—he becomes one with God, and the end of God in the man's creation, the end for which Jesus was born and died, is gained.

But I would not be supposed, from what I have said, to imagine the Lord without sympathy for the sorrows and pains which reveal what sin is, and by means of which He would make men sick of sin. With everything human He sympathizes. Evil is not human; it is the defect and opposite of the human; but the suffering that follows it is human, belonging of necessity to the human that has sinned. While it is by cause of sin, suffering is *for* the sinner, that he may be delivered from his sin.

Jesus is in Himself aware of every human pain. He feels it also. In Him, too, it is pain. With the energy of tenderest love He wills his brothers and sisters free, that He may fill them to overflowing with that essential thing, joy. For that they were indeed created. But the moment they exist, truth becomes the first thing, not happiness; and He must make them true.

Were it possible, however, for pain to continue after evil was gone, He would never rest while one ache was yet in the world. Perfect in sympathy, He feels in Himself, I say, the tortured presence of every nerve that lacks its repose. The man may recognize the evil in him only as pain; he may know little and care nothing about his sins; yet is the Lord sorry for his pain. He cries aloud, "Come unto me, all ye that labor and are heavy laden, and I will give you rest."

He does not say, "Come unto me, all ye that feel the burden of your sins." He opens His arms to all weary enough to come to Him in the poorest hope of rest. Right gladly would He free them from their misery—but He knows only one way: He will teach them to be like Himself, meek and lowly, bearing with gladness the yoke of His Father's will. This is the one, the only right, the only possible way of freeing them from their sins, the cause of their unrest. With them the weariness comes first; with Him the sins: there is but one cure for both—the will of the Father.

The disobedient and selfish would fain in the hell of their hearts possess the liberty and gladness that belong to purity and love, but they cannot have them; they are weary and heavy-laden, both with what they are, and because of what they were made for but are not. The Lord knows what they need; they know only what they want. They want ease; He knows they need purity.

Understanding through Obedience

It may be my reader will desire me to say *how* the Lord will deliver him from his sins. That is like the lawyer's "Who is my neighbor?" The spirit of such a mode of receiving the offer of the Lord's deliverance is the root of all the horrors of a corrupt theology, so acceptable to those who love weak and beggarly hornbooks of religion. Such questions spring from the passion for the fruit of the tree of knowledge, not the fruit of the tree of life. Men would understand: they do not care to *obey*—understand where it is impossible they should understand save by obeying.

For the sake of knowing, they postpone that which alone can enable them to know. They will not accept, that is, act upon, their highest privilege, that of obeying the Son of God. It is on them that do His will that the day dawns; to them the day-star arises in their hearts. Obedience is the soul of knowledge.

By obedience, I intend no kind of obedience to man or submission to authority claimed by man or community of men. I mean obedience to the will of the Father, however revealed in our conscience.

God forbid I should seem to despise understanding. The

New Testament is full of urgings to understand. Our whole life, to be life at all, must be a growth in understanding. What I cry out upon is the misunderstanding that comes of man's endeavor to understand while not obeying. Upon obedience our energy must be spent; understanding will follow.

Not anxious to know our duty, or knowing it and not doing it, how shall we understand that which only a true heart and a clean soul can ever understand? The power in us that would understand were it free, lies in the bonds of imperfection and impurity, and is therefore incapable of judging the divine. It cannot see the truth. If it could see it, it would not know it, and would not have it. Until a man begins to obey, the light that is in him is darkness.

Any honest soul may understand this much, however—for it is a thing we may of ourselves judge to be right—that the Lord cannot save a man from his sins while he holds to his sins. It is but common sense that a man, longing to be freed from suffering, or made able to bear it, should betake himself to the Power by whom he is. Equally is it common sense that, if a man would be delivered from the evil in him, he must himself begin to cast it out, himself begin to disobey it, and work righteousness. It is also common sense that a man should look for and expect the help of his Father in the endeavor. Alone, he might labor to all eternity and not succeed. He who has not made himself cannot set himself right without Him who made him. But his Maker is in him, and is his strength.

He cannot make himself pure, but he can leave that which is impure; he cannot save himself, but he can let the Lord save him. The struggle of his weakness is as essential to the coming victory as the strength of Him who resisted unto death, striving against sin.

The sum of the whole matter is this: the Son has come from the Father to set the children free from their sins; the children must hear and obey Him, that He may send forth judgment unto victory.

2
THE REMISSION OF SINS

"John the baptizer appeared in the wilderness, preaching a baptism of repentance for the forgiveness of sins."
Mark 1:4.

God and man must combine for salvation from sin, and the same word, here and elsewhere translated *remission* [i.e., in the KJV; *forgiveness* in the RSV], seems to be employed in the New Testament for the share of both in the great deliverance. Both God and man send away sins, but in the one case God sends away the sins of the man, and in the other the man sends away his own sins. That the phrase here intends repentance unto the ceasing from sin, the giving up of what is wrong, I will try to show at least probable.

Prepare the Way of the Lord
In the first place, the user of the phrase either defines the change of mind he means as one that has for its object the pardon of God, or as one that reaches to a new life: the latter seems to me the more natural interpretation by far. The kind and scope of the repentance or change, and not any end to be gained by it, appears intended. The change must be one of will and conduct—a radical change of life on the

21

part of the man: he must repent—that is, change his mind—not to a different opinion, not even to a mere betterment of his conduct—not to anything less than a sending away of sins.

Next, in St. Matthew's gospel, the Baptist's buttressing argument, or imminent motive for the change he is pressing upon the people, is that the kingdom of heaven is at hand: "Because the King of heaven is coming, you must give up your sinning." The same argument for immediate action lies in his quotation from Isaiah: "Prepare ye the way of the Lord; make straight in the desert a highway for our God." The only true, the only possible preparation for the coming Lord, is to cease from doing evil, and begin to do well—to send away sin.

Again, observe that, when the Pharisees came to John, he said to them, "Bear fruits that befit repentance": is not this the same as, "Repent unto the sending away of your sins"?

Note also, that, when the multitudes came to the prophet, and all—along with the classes most obnoxious to the rest, the publicans and the soldiers—asked what he would have them do, his instruction was throughout in the same direction: they must send away their sins, and each must begin with the fault that lay next to him. The kingdom of heaven was at hand; they must prepare the way of the Lord by beginning to do as must be done in His kingdom.

They could not rid themselves of their sins, but they could set about sending them away; they could quarrel with them, and proceed to turn them out of the house: the Lord was on His way to do His part in their final banishment. Those who had repented to the sending away of their sins, He would baptize with a holy power to send them away indeed. The operant will to get rid of them would be baptized with a fire that should burn them up.

I think, then, that the part of the repentant man, and not the part of God, in sending away of sins, is intended here. It is the man's one preparation for receiving the power to overcome them, the baptism of fire.

Real Existence

Not seldom, what comes in the name of the gospel of Jesus Christ must seem, even to one not far from the kingdom of heaven, no good news at all. It does not draw him; it wakes in him not a single hope. He has no desire after what it offers him as redemption. The God it gives him news of is not one to whom he would draw nearer. But when such a man comes to see that the very God must be his life, the heart of his consciousness; when he perceives that, rousing himself to put from him what is evil, and do the duty that lies at his door, he may fearlessly claim the help of Him who "loved him into being," then his will immediately sides with his conscience; he begins to try to *be*; and—first thing toward being—to rid himself of what is antagonistic to all being, namely, *wrong*.

Multitudes will not even approach the appalling task, the labor and pain of *being*. God is doing His part, is undergoing the mighty toil of an age-long creation, endowing men with power to be; but few as yet are those who take up their part, who respond to the call of God, who will to be, who put forth a divine effort after real existence. To the many the spirit of the prophet cries, "Turn ye, and change your way! The kingdom of heaven is near you. Let your King possess His own. Let God throne Himself in you, that His liberty be your life, and you free men. That He may enter, clear the house for Him. Send away the bad things out of it. Depart from evil, and do good. The duty that lieth at thy door, do it, be it great or small."

For indeed in this region there is no great or small. "Be content with your wages," said the Baptist to the soldiers. To many people now, the word would be, "Rule your temper"; or "Be courteous to all"; or, "Let each hold the other better than himself", or, "Be just to your neighbor that you may love him." We must bestir ourselves in the very spot on which we stand.

Understanding Christ's Baptism

We shall now, perhaps, be able to understand the relation of the Lord Himself to the baptism of John.

He came to John to be baptized; and most would say John's baptism was of repentance for the remission or pardon of sins. But the Lord could not be baptized for the remission of sins, for He had never done a selfish, an untrue, or an unfair thing. He needed no forgiveness; there was nothing to forgive. No more could He be baptized for repentance: in Him repentance would have been to turn to evil! Where, then, was the propriety of His coming to be baptized by John, and insisting on being by him baptized? It must lie elsewhere.

If we take the words of John to mean "the baptism of repentance unto the sending away of sins"; and if we bear in mind that in His case repentance could not be, inasmuch as what repentance is necessary to bring about in man was already existent in Jesus; then, altering the words to fit the case, and saying, "the baptism of willed devotion to the sending away of sin," we shall see at once how the baptism of Jesus was a thing right and fit.

That He had no sin to repent of, was not because He was so constituted that He could not sin if He would; it was because, of His own will and judgment, He sent sin away from Him—sent it from Him with the full choice and energy of His nature. God knows good and evil, and, blessed be His name, chooses good. Never will His righteous anger make Him unfair to us, make Him forget that we are dust. Like Him, His Son also chose good, and in that choice resisted all temptation to help His fellows otherwise than as their and His Father would.

Instead of crushing the power of evil by divine force; instead of compelling justice and destroying the wicked; instead of making peace on the earth by the rule of a perfect prince; instead of gathering the children of Jerusalem under His wings whether they would or not, and saving them from the horrors that anguished His prophetic soul—He let evil work its will while it lived; He contented himself with the slow unencouraging ways of help essential; making men good; casting out, not merely controlling Satan; carrying to their perfect issue on earth the old primeval principles because of which the Father honored Him: "You love righteousness and hate wickedness. Therefore God, your God, has anointed you with the oil of gladness above your fellows."

To love righteousness is to make it grow, not to avenge it; and to win for righteousness the true victory, He, as well as His brethren, had to send away evil. Throughout His life on earth, He resisted every impulse to work more rapidly for a lower good—strong, perhaps, when He saw old age and innocence and righteousness trodden under foot.

What but this gives any worth of reality to the temptation in the wilderness, to the devil's departing from Him for a season, to his coming again to experience a like failure? Ever and ever, in the whole attitude of His being, in His heart always lifted up, in His unfailing readiness to pull with the Father's yoke, He was repelling, driving away sin —away from Himself, and, as Lord of men, and their savior, away from others also, bringing them to abjure it like Himself.

No man, least of all any lord of men, can be good without willing to be good, without setting himself against evil, without sending away sin. Other men have to send it away out of them; the Lord had to send it away from before Him, that it should not enter into Him. Therefore is the stand against sin common to the Captain of salvation and the soldiers under Him.

The Holy War

What did Jesus come into the world to do? The will of God in saving His people from their sins—not from the punishment of their sins, that blessed aid to repentance, but from their sins themselves, the paltry as well as the heinous, the venial as well as the loathsome. His whole work was and is to send away sin—to banish it from the earth, yea, to cast it into the abyss of non-existence behind the back of God. His was the holy war; He came carrying it into our world; He resisted unto blood; the soldiers that followed Him He taught and trained to resist also unto blood, striving against sin; so He became the Captain of their salvation, and they, freed themselves, fought and suffered for others.

Such, then, as were baptized by John, were initiated into the company of those whose work was to send sin out of the world, and first, by sending it out of themselves, by having done with it. Their earliest endeavor in this direction would, as I have said, open the door for that help to enter without which a man could never succeed in the divinely arduous task—could not, because the region in which the work has to be wrought lies in the very roots of his own being, where, knowing nothing of the secrets of his essential existence, he can immediately do nothing, where the Maker of him alone is potent, alone is consciously present.

The change that must pass in him more than equals a new creation, inasmuch as it is a higher creation. But its necessity is involved in a former creation; and thence we have a right to ask help of our Creator, for He requires of us what He has created us unable to effect without Him.

Until a man become the power of his own existence, become his own God, the sole thing necessary to his existing is the will of God; for the well-being and perfecting of that existence, the sole thing necessary is, that the man should know his Maker present in him. All that the children want is their Father.

The one true end of all speech concerning holy things is —the persuading of the individual man to cease to do evil, to set himself to do well, to look to the Lord of his life to be on his side in the new struggle. Supposing the suggestions I have made correct, I do not care that my reader should understand them, except it be to turn against the evil in him, and begin to cast it out. If this be not the result, it is of no smallest consequence whether he agree with my interpretation or not. If he do thus repent, it is of equally little consequence; for, setting himself to do the truth, he is on the way to know all things. Real knowledge has begun to grow possible for him.

3

JESUS
IN THE WORLD

"Son, why have you treated us so?
Behold, your father and I have been looking
for you anxiously." And he
said to them, "How is it that you sought me?
Did you not know that
I must be in my Father's house?"
Luke 2:48-50.

Was that His saying? Why did they not understand it? Do
we understand it? What did His saying mean? The Greek
is not absolutely clear. Whether the Syriac words He used
were more precise, who in this world can tell? But had we
heard His very words, we too, with His father and mother,
would have failed to understand them. Must we fail still?

Let us see what lies in the Greek to guide us to the
thought in the mind of the Lord when He thus reasoned
with the apprehensions of His father and mother. The
Greek, taken literally, says, "Did you not know that I must
be in the _____ of my Father?" The authorized version supplies *business*; the revised, *house*. There is no noun
in the Greek, and the article "the" is in the plural. To trans-
late it as literally as it can be translated, making of it an
English sentence, the saying stands, "Did you not know
that I must be in the things of my Father?"

The plural article implies the English *things*; and the
question is then, What *things* does He mean? The word

might mean *affairs* or *business*; but why the plural article should be contracted to mean *house*, I do not know. In a great wide sense, no doubt, the word *house* might be used, as I am about to show, but surely not as meaning the temple.

He was arguing for confidence in God on the part of His parents, not for a knowledge of His whereabout. The same thing that made them anxious concerning Him prevented them from understanding His words—lack, namely, of faith in the Father. This, the one thing He came into the world to teach men, those words were meant to teach His parents. They are spirit and life, involving the one principle by which men shall live. They hold the same core as His words to His disciples in the storm, "Where is your faith?"

Christ's Liberty Among His Father's Things

. . . the Lord meant to remind them, or rather to make them feel, for they had not yet learned the fact, that He was never away from home, could not be lost, as they had thought Him; that He was in His Father's house all the time, where no hurt could come to Him. "The things" about Him were the furniture and utensils of His home; He knew them all and how to use them. "I must be among my Father's belongings." The world was His home because it was His Father's house. He was not a stranger who did not know His way about in it. He was no lost child, but with His Father all the time.

Here we find one main thing wherein the Lord differs from us: we are not at home in this great universe, our Father's house. We ought to be, and one day we shall be, but we are not yet. This reveals Jesus more than man, by revealing Him more man than we. We are not complete men, we are not anything near it, and are therefore out of harmony, more or less, with everything in the house of our birth and habitation.

Always struggling to make our home in the world, we

have not yet succeeded. We are not at home in it, because we are not at home with the lord of the house, the father of the family, not one with our elder brother who is his right hand. It is only the son, the daughter, that abideth ever in the house. When we are true children, if not the world, then the universe will be our home, felt and known as such, the house we are satisfied with, and would not change.

Hence, until then, the hard struggle, the constant strife we hold with *Nature*—as we call the things of our Father— a strife invaluable for our development, at the same time manifesting us not yet men enough to be lords of the house built for us to live in. We cannot govern or command in it as did the Lord, because we are not at one with His Father, therefore neither in harmony with His things, nor rulers over them. Our best power in regard to them is but to find out wonderful facts concerning them and their relations, and turn these facts to our uses on systems of our own.

How Christ Was at Home

Think for a moment how Jesus was at home among the things of His Father. It seems to me, I repeat, a spiritless explanation of His words—that the temple was the place where naturally He was at home. Does He make the least lamentation over the temple? It is Jerusalem He weeps over—the men of Jerusalem, the killers, the stoners. What was His place of prayer? Not the temple, but the moun-tain-top.

Where does He find symbols whereby to speak of what goes on in the mind and before the face of His Father in heaven? Not in the temple; not in its rites; not on its altars; not in its holy of holies; He finds them in the world and its lovely-lowly facts; on the roadside, in the field, in the vine-yard, in the garden, in the house; in the family, and the commonest of its affairs—the lighting of the lamp, the leav-ening of the meal, the neighbor's borrowing, the losing of the coin, the straying of the sheep. Even in the unlovely facts also of the world which He turns to holy use—such as the unjust judge, the false steward, the faithless laborers—He ignores the temple.

The world has for Him no chamber of terror. He walks to the door of the sepulcher, the sealed cellar of His Father's house, and calls forth its four-days dead. He rebukes the mourners, He stays the funeral, and gives back the departed children to their parents' arms. The roughest of its servants do not make Him wince; none of them are so arrogant as to disobey His word; He falls asleep in the midst of the storm that threatens to swallow His boat. Hear how, on that same occasion, He rebukes his disciples! The children to tremble at a gust of wind in the house! God's little ones afraid of the storm! Hear Him tell the watery floor to be still . . . .

All His life He was among His Father's things, either in heaven or in the world . . . . He claimed none of them as His own, would not have had one of them His except through His Father. Did He ever say, "This is mine, not yours"? Did He not say, "All things are mine, therefore they are yours"? That the things were His Father's made them precious things to Him. Oh, for His liberty among the things of the Father! Only by knowing them the things of our Father can we escape enslaving ourselves to them.

Through the false, the infernal idea of *having,* of *possessing* them, we make them our tyrants, make the relation between them and us an evil thing. The world was a blessed place to Jesus, because everything in it was His Father's. What pain must it not have been to Him, to see His brothers so vilely misuse the Father's house by grasping, each for himself, at the family things! If the knowledge that a spot in the landscape retains in it some pollution suffices to disturb our pleasure in the whole, how must it not have been with Him, how must it not be with Him now, in regard to the disfigurements and defilements caused by the greed of men, by their haste to be rich, in His Father's lovely house!

We too Shall Inherit the Earth

Jesus then, would have His parents understand that He was in His Father's world among His Father's things, where was nothing to hurt Him. He knew them all, was in the secret of them all, could use and order them as did His Father. To this same I think all we humans are destined to rise. Though so many of us now are ignorant what kind of home we need, what a home we are capable of having, we too shall inherit the earth with the Son eternal, doing with it as we would—willing with the will of the Father. To such a home as we now inhabit, only perfected, and perfectly beheld, we are traveling—never to reach it save by the obedience that makes us the children, therefore the heirs, of God. And, thank God! there the Father does not die that the children may inherit; for, bliss of heaven! we inherit with the Father.

4

JESUS AND
HIS FELLOW TOWNSMEN

"And he came to Nazareth, where he had been
brought up; and he went to the
synagogue, as his custom was, on the
sabbath day. And he stood up
to read; and there was given to him the book
of the prophet Isaiah. He opened
the book and found the place where it
was written, 'The Spirit of the Lord
is upon me, because he has anointed
me to preach good news to the poor.
He has sent me to proclaim release to the
captives and recovering of sight
to the blind, to set at liberty those
who are oppressed, to proclaim the
acceptable year of the Lord.'
And he closed the book, and gave it back
to the attendant, and sat down;
and the eyes of all in the synagogue were
fixed on him. And he began to
say to them, 'Today this scripture has
been fulfilled in your hearing.' "
Luke 4:16-21.

The point at which the Lord stops in His reading is suggestive: He closes the book, leaving the words "and the day of vengeance of our God," or, as in the Septuagint, "the day of recompense," unread: God's vengeance is as holy a thing as His love, yea, is love, for God is love and God is not

33

vengeance; but, apparently, the Lord would not give the word a place in His announcement of His mission: His hearers would not recognize it as a form of the Father's love, but as vengeance on their enemies, not vengeance on the selfishness of those who would not be their brother's keeper.

He had not begun with Nazareth, neither with Galilee. "A prophet has no honor in his own country," He said, and began to teach where it was more likely He would be heard. It is true that He wrought his first miracle in Cana, but that was at His mother's request, not of His own intent, and He did not begin His teaching there. He went first to Jerusalem, there cast out the buyers and sellers from the temple, and did other notable things alluded to by St. John; then went back to Galilee, where, having seen the things He did in Jerusalem, His former neighbors were now prepared to listen to Him.

Of these the Nazarenes, to whom the sight of Him was more familiar, retained the most prejudice against Him: He belonged to their very city! they had known Him from a child!—and low, indeed, are they in whom familiarity with the high and true breeds contempt! They are judged already. Yet such was the fame of the new prophet, that even they were willing to hear in the synagogue what He had to say to them—thence to determine for themselves what claim He had to an honorable reception.

But the eye of their judgment was not single, therefore was their body full of darkness. Should Nazareth indeed prove, to their self-glorifying satisfaction, the city of the great Prophet, they were more than ready to grasp at the renown of having produced Him: He was indeed the great Prophet, and within a few minutes they would have slain Him for the honor of Israel. In the ignoble even the love of their country partakes largely of the ignoble.

The Gospel Indeed
There was a shadow of the hateless vengeance of God in the

expulsion of the dishonest dealers from the temple with which the Lord initiated His mission: that was His first parable to Jerusalem; to Nazareth He comes with the sweetest words of the prophet of hope in His mouth—good tidings of great joy—of healing and sight and liberty; followed by the godlike announcement, that what the prophet had promised He was come to fulfil. His heart, His eyes, His lips, His hands—His whole body is full of gifts for men, and that day was that Scripture fulfilled in their ears.

The prophecy had gone before that He should save His people from their sins; He brings an announcement they will better understand: He is come, He says, to deliver men from sorrow and pain, ignorance and oppression, everything that makes life hard and unfriendly. What a gracious speech, what a daring pledge to a world whelmed in tyranny and wrong!

Every one will, I presume, confess to more or less misery. Its apparent source may be this or that; its real source is, to use a poor figure, a dislocation of the juncture between the created and the creating life. This primal evil is the parent of evils unnumbered, hence of miseries multitudinous, under the weight of which the arrogant man cries out against life, and goes on to misuse it, while the child looks around for help—and who shall help him but his Father! The Father is with him all the time, but it may be long ere the child knows himself in His arms.

The gospel according to this or that expounder of it may repel him unspeakably; the gospel according to Jesus Christ attracts him supremely, and ever holds where it has drawn him. To the priest, the scribe, the elder, exclaiming against his self-sufficiency in refusing what they teach, he answers, "It is life or death to me. Your gospel I cannot take. To believe as you would have me believe would be to lose my God. Your God is no God to me. I do not desire Him. I would rather die the death than believe in such a God. In the name of the true God, I cast your gospel from me; it is no gospel, and to believe it would be to wrong Him in whom alone lies my hope."

"But to believe in such a man," he might go on to say, "with such a message as I read of in the New Testament, is life from the dead. I have yielded myself, to live no more in the idea of self, but with the life of God. To Him I commit the creature He has made, that He may live in it, and work out its life—develop it according to the idea of it in His own creating mind. I fall in with His ways for me. I believe in Him. I trust Him. I try to obey Him. I look to be rendered capable of and receive a pure vision of His will, freedom from the prison-house of my limitation, from the bondage of a finite existence. For the finite that dwells in the infinite, and in which the infinite dwells, is finite no longer."

"Those who are thus children indeed, are little Gods, the divine brood of the infinite Father. No mere promise of deliverance from the consequences of sin would be any gospel to me. Less than the liberty of a holy heart, less than the freedom of the Lord himself, will never satisfy one human soul. Father, set me free in the glory of thy will, so that I will only as thou willest. Thy will be at once thy perfection and mine. Thou alone art deliverance—absolute safety from every cause and kind of trouble that ever existed, anywhere now exists, or ever can exist in thy universe."

The Attitude of the Nazarenes
But the people of the Lord's town, to whom He read, appropriating them, the gracious words of the prophet, were of the wise and prudent of their day. With one and the same breath they seem to cry, "These things are good, it is true, but they must come after our way. We must have the promise to our fathers fulfilled—that we shall rule the world, the chosen of God, the children of Abraham and Israel. We want to be a free people, manage our own affairs, live in plenty, and do as we please. Liberty alone can ever cure the woes of which you speak. We do not need to be better; we are well enough. Give us riches and honor, and keep us content with ourselves, that we may be satisfied with our

own likeness, and thou shalt be the Messiah." Never, perhaps, would such be men's spoken words, but the prevailing condition of their minds might often well take form in such speech.

But the Lord knew what was in their hearts; He knew the false notion with which they were almost ready to declare for Him; He knew also the final proof to which they were in their wisdom and prudence about to subject Him. He did not look likely to be a prophet, seeing He had grown up among them, and had never shown any credentials: they had a right to proof positive! They had heard of wonderful things He had done in other places: why had they not first of all been done in *their* sight? Who had a claim equal to theirs? who so capable as they to pronounce judgment on His mission whether false or true: had they not known Him from childhood? His words were gracious, but words were nothing: He must *do* something—something wonderful! Without such conclusive, satisfying proof, Nazareth would never acknowledge Him!

They were not a gracious people, or a good. The Lord saw their thought, and it was far from being to His mind. He desired no such reception as they were at present equal to giving a prophet. His mighty works were not meant for such as they—to convince them of what they were incapable of understanding or welcoming! Those who would not believe without signs and wonders could never believe worthily with any number of them, and none should be given them!

His mighty works were to rouse the love and strengthen the faith of the meek and lowly in heart, of such as were ready to come to the light, and show that they were of the light. He knew how poor the meaning the Nazarenes put on the words He had read; what low expectations they had of the Messiah when most they longed for His coming. They did not hear the prophet while He read the prophet!

Salvation from their sins was not in their hearts, not in their imaginations, not at all in their thoughts. They had heard Him read His commission to heal the broken-hearted; they would rush to break hearts in His name. The Lord knew them and their vain expectations. He would have no such followers—no followers on false conceptions —no followers whom wonders would delight but nowise better! The Nazarenes were not yet of the sort that needed but one change to be His people. He had come to give them help; until they accepted His, they could have none to give Him.

The Worst Insult

The Lord saw them on the point of challenging a display of His power, and anticipated the challenge with a refusal.

For the better understanding of His words, let me presume to paraphrase them: "I know you will apply to me the proverb, Physician, heal thyself, requiring me to prove what is said of me in Capernaum, by doing the same here; but there is another proverb, No prophet is accepted in his own country. Unaccepted I do nothing wonderful. In the great famine, Elijah was sent to no widow of the many in Israel, but to a Sidonian; and Elisha cured no leper of the many in Israel, but Naaman the Syrian. There are those fit to see signs and wonders; they are not always the kin of the prophet."

The Nazarenes heard with indignation. Their wonder at His gracious words was changed to bitterest wrath. The very beams of their ugly religion were party-spirit, exclusiveness, and pride in the fancied favor of God for them only of all the nations: to hint at the possibility of a revelation of the glory of God to a stranger; far more, to hint that a stranger might be fitter to receive such a revelation than a Jew, was an offense reaching to the worst insult; and it was cast in their teeth by a common man of their own city! "Thou art but a well-known carpenter's son, and dost thou teach *us*! Darest thou imply a divine preference for Capernaum over Nazareth?"

How could there be any miracle for such! They were well

satisfied with themselves, and

> Nothing almost sees miracles
> But misery.

Need and the upward look, the mood ready to believe when and where it can, the embryonic faith, is dear to Him whose love would have us trust Him. Let any man seek Him —not in curious inquiry whether the story of Him may be true or cannot be true, but in humble readiness to accept Him altogether if only he can— and he shall find Him; we shall not fail of help to believe because we doubt. But if the questioner be such that the dispersion of his doubt would but leave him in disobedience, the Power of truth has no care to effect his conviction.

Why cast out a devil that the man may the better do the work of the devil? The Lord could easily have satisfied the Nazarenes that He was the Messiah: they would but have hardened into the nucleus of an army for the subjugation of the world. To a warfare with their own sins, to the subjugation of their doing and desiring to do the will of the great Father, all the miracles in His power would never have persuaded them. A true convincement is not possible to hearts and minds like theirs. Not only is it impossible for a low man to believe a thousandth part of what a noble man can, but a low man cannot believe anything as a noble man believes it.

The men of Nazareth could have believed in Jesus as their savior from the Romans. As their savior from their sins they could not believe in Him, for they loved their sins. The King of heaven came to offer them a share in His kingdom; but they were not poor in spirit, and the kingdom of heaven was not for them. Gladly would they have inherited the earth; but they were not meek, and the earth was for the lowly children of the perfect Father.

5

THE HEIRS OF HEAVEN AND EARTH

*"And He opened his mouth and taught them,
saying, Blessed are the poor
in spirit; for theirs is the kingdom of
heaven . . . . Blessed are the meek;
for they shall inherit the earth."*
Matthew 5:2, 3, 5.

The words of the Lord are the seed sown by the sower. Into our hearts they must fall that they may grow. Meditation and prayer must water them, and obedience keep them in the sunlight. Thus will they bear fruit for the Lord's gathering.

Those of His disciples, that is, obedient hearers, who had any experience in trying to live, would, in part, at once understand them; but as they obeyed and pondered, the meaning of them would keep growing. This we see in the writings of the apostles. It will be so with us also, who need to understand everything He said neither more nor less than they to whom first He spoke; while our obligation to understand is far greater than theirs at the time, inasmuch as we have had nearly two thousand years' experience of the continued coming of the kingdom He then preached: it is not yet come; it has been all the time, and is now, drawing slowly nearer.

The sermon on the mount, as it is commonly called,

seems the Lord's first free utterance, in the presence of any large assembly, of the good news of the kingdom. How different, at the first sound of it, must the good news have been from the news anxiously expected by those who waited for the Messiah! Even the Baptist in prison lay listening after something of quite another sort. The Lord had to send him a message, by eye-witnesses of His doings, to remind him that God's thoughts are not as our thoughts, or His ways as our ways—that the design of God is other and better than the expectation of men.

His summary of the gifts He was giving to men culminated with the preaching of the good news to the poor. If John had known these His doings before, he had not recognized them as belonging to the Lord's special mission: the Lord tells him it is not enough to have accepted Him as the Messiah; he must recognize His doings as the work He had come into the world to do, and as in their nature so divine as to be the very business of the Son of God in whom the Father was well pleased.

Wherein then consisted the goodness of the news which He opened His mouth to give them? What was in the news to make the poor glad? Why was His arrival with such words in His heart and mouth the coming of the kingdom?

The Good News of Uplifting Love

All good news from heaven is of *truth*—essential truth, involving duty, and giving and promising help to the performance of it. There can be no good news for us men, except of uplifting love, and no one can be lifted up who will not rise. If God Himself sought to raise His little ones without their consenting effort, they would drop from His foiled endeavor. He will carry us in His arms till we are able to walk; He will carry us in His arms when we are weary with walking; He will not carry us if we will not walk.

The good news of Jesus was just the news of the thoughts and ways of the Father in the midst of His family. He told them that the way men thought for themselves and their children was not the way God thought for Himself and His children; that the kingdom of heaven was founded, and must at length show itself founded, on very different principles from those of the kingdoms and families of the world, meaning by the world that part of the Father's family which will not be ordered by Him, will not even try to obey Him.

The world's man, its great, its successful, its honorable man, is he who may have and do what he pleases, whose strength lies in money and the praise of men. The greatest in the kingdom of heaven is the man who is humblest and serves his fellows the most. Multitudes of men, in no degree notable as ambitious or proud, hold the ambitious, the proud man in honor, and, for all deliverance, hope after some shadow of his prosperity. How many even of those who look for the world to come seek to the powers of this world for deliverance from its evils, as if God were the God of the world to come only! The oppressed of the Lord's time looked for a Messiah to set their nation free, and make it rich and strong; the oppressed of our time believe in money, knowledge, and the will of a people which needs but power to be in its turn the oppressor. The first words of the Lord on this occasion were: "Blessed are the poor in spirit, for theirs is the kingdom of heaven."

The Poor in Spirit

The Son of God will favor no smallest ambition, be it in the heart of him who leans on His bosom. The kingdom of God, the refuge of the oppressed, the golden age of the new world, . . . the home of the children, will not open its gates to the most miserable who would rise above his equal in misery, who looks down on any one more miserable than himself. It is the home of perfect brotherhood.

The poor, the beggars in spirit, the humble men of heart, the unambitious, the unselfish; those who never despise men, and never seek their praises; the lowly, who see nothing to admire in themselves, therefore cannot seek to be admired of others; the men who give themselves away

—these are the freemen of the kingdom, these are the citizens of the new Jerusalem.

The men who are aware of their own essential poverty; not the men who are poor in friends, poor in influence, poor in acquirements, poor in money, but those who are poor in spirit, who *feel themselves poor creatures*; who know nothing to be pleased with themselves for, and desire nothing to make them think well of themselves; who know that they need much to make their life worth living, to make their existence a good thing, to make them fit to live; these humble ones are the poor whom the Lord calls blessed.

When a man says, I am low and worthless, then the gate of the kingdom begins to open to him, for there enter the true, and this man has begun to know the truth concerning himself. Whatever such a man has attained to, he straightway forgets; it is part of him and behind him. His business is with what he has not, with the things that lie above and before him.

The man who is proud of anything he thinks he has reached, has not reached it. He is but proud of himself, and imagining a cause for his pride. If he had reached, he would already have begun to forget. He who delights in contemplating whereto he has attained, is not merely sliding back; he is already in the dirt of self-satisfaction. The gate of tne kingdom is closed, and he outside.

The man who does not house self has room to be his real self—God's eternal idea of him. He lives eternally; in virtue of the creative power present in him with momently unimpeded creation, he *is*. How should there be in him one thought of ruling or commanding or surpassing! He can imagine no bliss, no good in being greater than some one else.

He is unable to wish himself other then he is, except more what God made him for, which is indeed the highest willing of the will of God. His brother's well-being is essential to bliss. The thought of standing higher in the favor of God than his brother would make him miserable. He would lift every brother to the embrace of the Father. Blessed are the poor in spirit, for they are of the same spirit as God, and of nature the kingdom of heaven is theirs.

The Meek
"Blessed are the meek, for they shall inherit the earth," expresses the same principle: the same law holds in the earth as in the kingdom of heaven. How should it be otherwise? Has the Creator of the ends of the earth ceased to rule it after His fashion, because His rebellious children have so long, to their own hurt, vainly endeavored to rule it after theirs? The kingdom of heaven belongs to the poor; the meek shall inherit the earth.

The earth as God sees it, as those to whom the kingdom of heaven belongs also see it, is good, all good, very good, fit for the meek to inherit; and one day they shall inherit it—not indeed as men of the world count inheritance, but as the Maker and Owner of the world has from the first counted it. So different are the two ways of inheriting, that one of the meek may be heartily enjoying his possession, while one of the proud is selfishly walling him out from the spot in it he loves best.

The meek are those that do not assert themselves, do not defend themselves, never dream of avenging themselves, or of returning aught but good for evil. They do not imagine it their business to take care of themselves. The meek man may indeed take much thought, but it will not be for himself. He never builds an exclusive wall, shuts any honest neighbor out. He will not always serve the wish, but always the good of his neighbor. His service must be true service. Because the man is meek, his eye is single; he sees things as God sees them, as He would have His child see them: to confront creation with pure eyes is to possess it.

True Possession
We cannot see the world as God means it, save in proportion as our souls are meek. In meekness only are we its in-

heritors. Meekness alone makes the spiritual retina pure to receive God's things as they are, mingling with them neither imperfection nor impurity of its own. A thing so beheld that it conveys to me the divine thought issuing in its form, is mine; by nothing but its mediation between God and my life can anything be mine.

The man so dull as to insist that a thing is his because he has bought it and paid for it, had better bethink himself that not all the combined forces of law, justice, and goodwill can keep it his; while even death cannot take the world from the man who possesses it as alone the Maker of him and it cares that he should possess it. This man leaves it, but carries it with him; that man carries with him only its loss.

In the soul of the meek, the earth remains an endless possession—his because He who made it is his—his as nothing but his Maker could ever be the creature's. He has the earth by his divine relation to Him who sent it forth from Him as a tree sends out its leaves. To inherit the earth is to grow ever more alive to the presence, in it and in all its parts, of Him who is the life of men. How far one may advance in such inheritance while yet in the body will simply depend on the meekness he attains while yet in the body; but it may be . . . that the new heavens and the new earth are the same in which we now live, righteously inhabited by the meek, with their deeper-opened eyes.

What if the meek of the dead be thus possessing it even now! But I do not care to speculate. It is enough that the man who refuses to assert himself, seeking no recognition by men, leaving the care of his life to the Father, and occupying himself with the will of the Father, shall find himself, by and by, at home in the Father's house, with all the Father's property his.

Which is more the possessor of the world—he who has a thousand houses, or he who, without one house to call his own, has ten in which his knock at the door would rouse instant jubilation? Which is the richer—the man who, his large money spent, would have no refuge; or he for whose necessity a hundred would sacrifice comfort? Which of the two possessed the earth—king Agrippa or tent-maker Paul?

The same spirit, then, is required for possessing the kingdom of heaven, and for inheriting the earth. How should it not be so, when the one Power is the informing life of both? If we are the Lord's, we possess the kingdom of heaven, and so inherit the earth. How many who call themselves by His name would have it otherwise: they would possess the earth and inherit the kingdom! Such fill churches and chapels on Sundays: anywhere suits for the worship of Mammon.

Yet verily, earth as well as heaven may be largely possessed even now.

Two men are walking abroad together. To the one, the world yields thought after thought of delight; he sees heaven and earth embrace one another; he feels an indescribable presence over and in them; his joy will afterward, in the solitude of his chamber, break forth in song. To the other, oppressed with the thought of his poverty, or ruminating how to make much into more, the glory of the Lord is but a warm summer day; it enters in at no window of his soul; it offers him no gift; for, in the very temple of God, he looks for no God in it.

Nor must there needs be two men to think and feel differently. In what diverse fashion will any one *subject* to ever-changing mood see the same world of the same glad Creator! Alas for men, if it changed as we change, if it grew meaningless when we grow faithless! Thought for a morrow that may never come, dread of the dividing death which works for endless companionship, anger with one we love, will cloud the radiant morning, and make the day dark with night.

At evening, having bethought ourselves, and returned to Him that feeds the ravens, and watches the dying sparrow, and says to His children, "Love one another," the sunset splendor is glad over us, the western sky is refulgent as

the court of the Father when the glad news is spread abroad
that a sinner has repented. We have mourned in the twi-
light of our little faith, but, having sent away our sin, the
glory of God's heaven over His darkening earth has comforted us.

6

SORROW
THE PLEDGE OF JOY

*"Blessed are those who mourn, for they
shall be comforted."*
Matthew 5:4.

There is no evil in sorrow. True, it is not an essential good,
a good in itself, like love; but it will mingle with any good
thing, and is even so allied to good that it will open the door
of the heart for any good.

It is true also that joy is in its nature more divine than
sorrow; for, although man must sorrow, and God share in
his sorrow, yet in Himself God is not sorrowful, and the
"glad Creator" never made man for sorrow: it is but a
stormy strait through which he must pass to His ocean of
peace.

Still, a man in sorrow is in general far nearer God than a
man in joy. Gladness may make a man forget his thanks-
giving; misery drives him to his prayers. For we *are* not yet,
we are only *becoming*. The endless day will at length dawn
whose every throbbing moment will heave our hearts God-
ward; we shall scarce need to lift them up: now, there are
two doorkeepers to the house of prayer, and Sorrow is
more on the alert to open than her grandson Joy.

49

The promise to them that mourn is not *the kingdom of heaven*, but that their mourning shall be ended, that they shall be comforted. To mourn is not to fight with evil; it is only to miss that which is good. It is not an essential heavenly condition, like poorness of spirit or meekness. No man will carry his mourning with him into heaven—or, if he does, it will speedily be turned either into joy, or into what will result in joy, namely, redemptive action.

The loss of the loved by death is the main cause of the mourning of the world. The Greek word here used to describe the blessed of the Lord generally means *those that mourn for the dead*. It is not in the New Testament employed excusively in this sense, neither do I imagine it stands here for such only: there are griefs sorer far than death, and harder far to comfort—harder even for God Himself, with whom all things are possible; but it may give pleasure to know that the promise of comfort to those that mourn may specially apply to those that mourn because their loved have gone out of their sight, and beyond the reach of their cry.

The Excellence of God's Comfort
"The Lord means of course," someone may say, "that the comfort of the mourners will be the restoration of that which they have lost. He means, 'Blessed are ye although ye mourn, for your sorrow will be turned into joy.' "

But would such restoration be comfort enough for the heart of Jesus to give? To call a man *blessed* in his sorrow because of something to be given him, surely implies a something better than what he had before!

True, the joy that is past may have been so great that the man might well feel blessed in the merest hope of its restoration; but would that be meaning enough for the word in the mouth of the Lord? That the interruption of his blessedness was but temporary would hardly be fit ground for calling the man *blessed* in the interruption. *Blessed* is a strong word, and in the mouth of Jesus means all it can mean. Can His saying here mean less than, "Blessed are they that mourn, for they shall be comforted with a bliss well worth all the pain of the medicinal sorrow"?

Besides, the benediction surely means that the man is blessed *because* of his condition of mourning, not in spite of it. His mourning is surely a part, at least, of the Lord's ground for congratulating him: is it not the present operative means whereby the consolation is growing possible? In a word, I do not think the Lord would be content to call a man blessed on the mere ground of his going to be restored to a former bliss by no means perfect. I think He congratulated the mourners upon the grief they were enduring, because He saw the excellent glory of the comfort that was drawing nigh; because He knew the immeasurably greater joy to which the sorrow was at once clearing the way and conducting the mourner.

When I say *greater*, God forbid I should mean *other*! I mean the same bliss, divinely enlarged and divinely purified—passed again through the hands of the creative Perfection. God's comfort must ever be larger than man's grief, else were there gaps in his Godhood. Mere restoration would leave a hiatus, barren and growthless, in the development of His children.

The Change God Will Make

We shall all doubtless be changed, but in what direction?—to something less, or to something greater?—to something that is less we, which means degradation? to something that is not we, which means annihilation? or to something that is more we, which means a further development of the original idea of us, the divine germ of us, holding in it all we ever were, all we ever can and must become?

Is it not of the very essence of the Christian hope, that we shall be changed from much bad to all good? If a wife so love that she would keep every opposition, every inconsistency in her husband's as yet but partially harmonious character, she does not love well enough for the kingdom of heaven. If its imperfections be essential to the individuality she loves, and to the repossession of her joy in it, she may be sure that, if he were restored to her as she would have him, she would soon come to love him less—perhaps to love him not at all; for no one who does not love perfection will ever keep constant in loving.

Fault is not lovable; it is only the good in which the alien fault dwells that causes it to seem capable of being loved. Neither is it any man's peculiarities that make him beloved; it is the essential humanity underlying those peculiarities. They may make him interesting, and, where not offensive, they may come to be loved for the sake of the man; but in themselves they are of smallest account.

We must not, however, confound peculiarity with diversity. Diversity is in and from God; peculiarity in and from man. The real man is the divine idea of him; the man God had in view when He began to send him forth out of thought into thinking; the man He is now working to perfect by casting out what is not he, and developing what is he.

But in God's real men, that is, His ideal men, the diversity is infinite; He does not repeat His creations; every one of His children differs from every other, and in every one the diversity is lovable. God gives in His children an analysis of Himself, an analysis that will never be exhausted. It is the original God-idea of the individual man that will at length be given, without spot or blemish, into the arms of love.

Such, surely, is the heart of the comfort the Lord will give those whose love is now making them mourn; and their present blessedness must be the expectation of the time when the true lover shall find the restored the same as the lost—with precious differences: the things that were not like the true self, gone or going; the things that were loveliest, lovelier still; the restored not merely more than the lost, but more the person lost than he or she that was lost. For the things which made him or her what he or she was, the things that rendered lovable, the things essential to the person, will be more present, because more developed.

Making Amends
There is one phase of our mourning for the dead which I must not leave unconsidered, seeing it is the pain within pain of all our mourning—the sorrow, namely, with its keen recurrent pangs, because of things we have said or done, or omitted to say or do, while we companied with the departed. Would God be perfect if in His restitution of all things there were no opportunity for declaring our bitter grief and shame for the past? no room for making amends?

At the same time, when the desired moment comes, one look in the eyes may be enough, and we shall know one another even as God knows us. Like the purposed words of the prodigal in the parable, it may be that the words of our confession will hardly find place. Heart may so speak to heart as to forget there were such things. Mourner, hope in God, and comfort where thou canst, and the Lord of mourners will be able to comfort thee the sooner. It may be thy very severity with thyself has already moved the Lord to take thy part.

The Perfection of God's Comfort
Whatever selfishness clouds the love that mourns the loss of love, that selfishness must be taken out of it—burned out of it even by pain extreme, if such be needful. Because of that in thy love which was not love, it may be thy loss has come; anyhow, because of thy love's defect, thou must suffer that it may be supplied. God will not, like the unjust judge, avenge thee to escape the cry that troubles Him. No crying will make Him comfort thy selfishness. He will not render thee incapable of loving truly. He despises neither thy love, though mingled with selfishness, nor thy suffering that springs from both; He will disentangle thy selfishness from thy love, and cast it into the fire.

His cure for thy selfishness at once and thy suffering is to make thee love more—and more truly; not with the love of love, but with the love of the person whose lost love thou bemoanest. For the love of love is the love of thyself.

Begin to love as God loves, and thy grief will assuage; but for comfort wait His time. What He will do for thee, He only knows. It may be thou wilt never know what He will do, but only what He has done: it was too good for thee to know save by receiving it. The moment thou art capable of it, thine it will be.

Whether or not the Lord was here thinking specially of the mourners for the dead, as I think He was, He surely does not limit the word of comfort to them, or wish us to believe less than that His Father has perfect comfort for every human grief. One thing is clear in regard to every trouble— that the natural way with it is straight to the Father's knee. The Father is father *for* His children, else why did He make Himself their father?

The Lord has come to wipe away our tears. He is doing it; He will have it done as soon as He can; and until He can, He would have them flow without bitterness; to which end He tells us it is a blessed thing to mourn, because of the comfort on its way. Accept His comfort now, and so prepare for the comfort at hand. He is getting you ready for it, but you must be a fellow-worker with Him, or He will never have done. He *must* have you pure in heart, eager after righteousness, a very child of His Father in heaven.

7

GOD'S FAMILY

*"Blessed are the pure in heart, for they
shall see God. Blessed
are those who hunger and thirst for
righteousness, for they shall
be satisfied. Blessed are the peacemakers,
for they shall be called sons of God."
Matthew 5:8, 6, 9.*

The cry of the deepest in man has always been to see God.
It was the cry of Moses and the cry of Job, the cry of psalmist
and of prophet; and to the cry there has ever been faintly
heard a far approach of coming answer. In the fullness of
time the Son appears with the proclamation that a certain
class of men shall behold the Father: "Blessed are the pure
in heart," He cries, "for they shall see God." He who saw
God, who sees Him now, who always will see Him, says,
"Be pure, and you also shall see Him."

To see God was the Lord's own, eternal, one happiness;
therefore He knew that the essential bliss of the creature
is to behold the face of the Creator. In that face lies the mystery of a man's own nature, the history of a man's own
being. He who can read no line of it can know neither himself nor his fellow; he only who knows God a little can at all
understand man. The blessed in Dante's Paradise ever and
always read each other's thoughts in God. Looking to Him,
they find their neighbor.

All that the creature needs to see or know, all that the creature can see or know, is the face of Him from whom he came. Not seeing and knowing it, he will never be at rest; seeing and knowing it, his existence will yet indeed be a mystery to him and an awe, but no more a dismay.

None but the pure in heart see God; only the growing-pure hope to see Him. Even those who saw the Lord, the express image of His person, did not see God. They only saw Jesus—and then but the outside Jesus, or a little more. They were not pure in heart; they saw Him and did not see Him. They saw Him with their eyes, but not with those eyes which alone can see God. Those were not born in them yet. Neither the eyes of the resurrection-body, nor the eyes of unembodied spirits can see God; only the eyes of that eternal something that is of the very essence of God, the thought-eyes, the truth-eyes, the love-eyes, can see Him.

It is not because we are created and He uncreated, it is not because of any difference involved in that difference of all differences, that we cannot see Him. If He pleased to take a shape, and that shape were presented to us, and we saw that shape, we should not therefore be seeing God. Even if we knew it was a shape of God—call it even God Himself our eyes rested upon; if we had been told the fact and believed the report; yet, if we did not see the *Godness*, . . . we should not be seeing God, we should only be seeing the tabernacle in which for the moment He dwelt. In other words, not seeing what in the form made it a form fit for Him to take, we should not be seeing a presence which could only be God.

To see God is to stand on the highest point of created being. Not until we see God—no partial and passing embodiment of Him, but the abiding presence—do we stand upon our own mountain-top, the height of the existence God has given us, and up to which He is leading us. That there we should stand, is the end of our creation.

This truth is at the heart of everything, means all kinds of completions, may be uttered in many ways; but language will never compass it, for form will never contain it. Nor shall we ever see, that is, know, God perfectly. We shall indeed never absolutely know man or woman or child; but we may know God as we never can know human being—as we never can know ourselves. We not only may, but we must so know Him, and it can never be until we are pure in heart. Then shall we know Him with the infinitude of an ever-growing knowledge.

Becoming Pure

"What is it, then, to be pure in heart?"

I answer: It is not necessary to define this purity, or to have in the mind any clear form of it. For even to know perfectly (were that possible) what purity of heart is, would not be to be pure in heart.

"How then am I to try after it? can I do so without knowing what it is?"

Though you do not know any definition of purity, you know enough to begin to be pure. You do not know what a man is, but you know how to make his acquaintance—perhaps even how to gain his friendship. Your brain does not know what purity is; your heart has some acquaintance with purity itself. Your brain is seeking to know what it is, may even obstruct your heart in bettering its friendship with it. To know what purity is, a man must already be pure; but he who can put the question already knows enough of purity, I repeat, to begin to become pure. If this moment you determine to start for purity, your conscience will at once tell you where to begin. If you reply, "My conscience says nothing definite," I answer, "You are but playing with your conscience. Determine, and it will speak."

If you care to see God, be pure. If you will not be pure, you will grow more and more impure; and instead of seeing God, will at length find yourself face to face with a vast inane—a vast inane, yet filled full of one inhabitant, that devouring monster, your own false self. If for this neither do you care, I tell you there is a Power that will not have it

so; a Love that will make you care by the consequences of
not caring.

Hungering after God

To hunger and thirst after anything implies a sore personal
need, a strong desire, a passion for that thing. Those that
hunger and thirst after righteousness seek with their whole
nature the design of that nature. Nothing less will give
them satisfaction; that alone will set them at ease. They long
to be delivered from their sins, to send them away, to be
clean and blessed by their absence—in a word, to become
men, God's men; for, sin gone, all the rest is good.

Righteousness itself, God's righteousness, rightness in
their own being, in heart and brain and hands, is what they
desire. Of such men was Nathanael, in whom was no guile;
such, perhaps, was Nicodemus too, although he did come
to Jesus by night; such was Zacchaeus. The temple could
do nothing to deliver them; but, by their very futility, its
observances had done their work, developing the desires
they could not meet, making the men hunger and thirst the
more after genuine righteousness: the Lord must bring
them this bread from heaven. With Him, the live, original
rightness, in their hearts, they must speedily become
righteous.

With that Love their friend, who is at once both the root
and the flower of things, they would strive vigorously as
well as hunger eagerly after righteousness. Love is the
father of righteousness. It could not be, and could not be
hungered after, but for love. The Lord of Righteousness
Himself could not live without Love, without the Father in
Him. Every heart was created for, and can live no otherwise
than in and upon love eternal, perfect, pure, unchanging;
and love necessitates righteousness.

In how many souls has not the very thought of a real God
waked a longing to be different, to be pure, to be right! The
fact that this feeling is possible, that a soul can become
dissatisfied with itself, and desire a change in itself, reveals

God as an essential part of its being; for in itself the soul is aware that it cannot be what it would, what it ought—that it cannot set itself right: a need has been generated in the soul for which the soul can generate no supply; a presence higher than itself must have caused that need; a power greater than itself must supply it, for the soul knows its very need, its very lack, is of something greater than itself.

But the primal need of the human soul is yet greater than this; the longing after righteousness is only one of the manifestations of it; the need. . . . is the man's need of God. A moral, that is, a human, a spiritual being, must either be God, or one with God. This truth begins to reveal itself when the man begins to feel that he cannot cast out the thing he hates, cannot be the thing he loves. That he hates thus, that he loves thus, is because God is in him, but he finds he has not enough of God. His awakening strength manifests itself in his sense of weakness, for only strength can know itself weak. The negative cannot know itself at all. Weakness cannot know itself weak. It is a little strength that longs for more; it is infant righteousness that hungers after righteousness.

Being Filled

To be filled with righteousness will be to forget even righteousness itself in the bliss of being righteous, that is, a child of God. The thought of righteousness will vanish in the fact of righteousness. When a creature is just what he is meant to be, what only he is fit to be; when, therefore, he is truly himself, he never thinks what he is. He *is* that thing; why think about it? It is no longer outside of him that he should contemplate or desire it.

God made man, and woke in him the hunger for righteousness; the Lord came to enlarge and rouse this hunger. The first and lasting effect of His words must be to make the hungering and thirsting long yet more. If their passion grow to a despairing sense of the unattainable, a hopelessness of ever gaining that without which life were worthless, let them remember that the Lord congratulates the hungry and the thirsty, so sure does He know them of being one day satisfied. Their hunger is a precious thing to have . . .

If your hunger seems long in being filled, it is well it should seem long. But what if your righteousness tarry because your hunger after it is not eager? There are those who sit long at the table because their desire is slow; they eat as who should say, We need no food. In things spiritual, increasing desire is the sign that satisfaction is drawing nearer.

Hear another like word of the Lord. He assures us that the Father hears the cries of His elect—of those whom He seeks to worship Him because they worship in spirit and in truth. "Shall not God avenge His own elect," He says, "which cry day and night unto Him?" Now what can God's elect have to keep on crying for night and day, but righteousness? He allows that God seems to put off answering them, but assures us He will answer them speedily.

Even now He must be busy answering their prayers; increasing hunger is the best possible indication that He is doing so. For some divine reason it is well they should not yet know in themselves that He is answering their prayers; but the day must come when we shall be righteous even as He is righteous; when no word of His will miss being understood because of our lack of righteousness; when no unrighteousness shall hide from our eyes the face of the Father.

Being Peacemakers

These two promises, of seeing God and being filled with righteousness, have place between the individual man and his Father in heaven directly; the promise I now come to has place between a man and his God as the God of other men also, as the Father of the whole family in heaven and earth: "Blessed are the peacemakers, for they shall be called the children of God."

Those that are on their way to see God, those who are

growing pure in heart through hunger and thirst after righteousness, are indeed the children of God; but specially the
Lord calls those His children who, on their way home, are
peacemakers in the traveling company; for, surely, those in
any family are specially the children, who make peace with
and among the rest.

The true idea of the universe is the whole family in heav-
en and earth. All the children in this part of it, the earth, at
least, are not good children; but however far, therefore, the
earth is from being a true portion of a real family, the life-
germ at the root of the world—that by and for which it exists
—is its relation to God the Father of men.

God, then, would make of the world a true, divine family. Now the primary necessity to the very existence of a
family is peace. Many a human family is no family, and the
world is no family yet, for the lack of peace. Wherever peace
is growing, there, of course, is the live peace, counteracting
disruption and disintegration, and helping the development of the true essential family.

The peacemakers . . . . are the true children of that family, the allies and ministers of every clasping and consoli-
dating force in it; fellow-workers they are with God in the
creation of the family; they help Him to get it to His mind,
to perfect His father-idea. Ever radiating peace, they wel-
come love, but do not seek it; they provoke no jealousy.
They are the children of God, for, like Him, they would be
one with His creatures.

His eldest Son, His very likeness, was the first of the
family peacemakers. Preaching peace to them that were
afar off and them that were nigh, He stood undefended in
the turbulent crowd of His fellows, and it was only over His
dead body that His brothers began to come together in the
peace that will not be broken. He rose again from the dead;
His peacemaking brothers, like Himself, are dying unto
sin; and not yet have the evil children made their Father
hate, or their Elder Brother flinch.

On the other hand, those whose influence is to divide

and separate, causing the hearts of men to lean away from each other, make themselves the children of the evil one: born of God and not of the devil, they turn from God, and adopt the devil their father. They set their God-born life against God, against the whole creative, redemptive purpose of His unifying will, ever obstructing the one prayer of the First-born—that the children may be one with Him in the Father.

Are we to treat persons known for liars and strifemakers as the children of the devil or not? Are we to turn away from them, and refuse to acknowledge them, rousing an ignorant strife of tongues concerning our conduct? Are we guilty of connivance, when silent as to the ambush whence we know the wicked arrow privily shot? Are we to call the traitor to account? or are we to give warning of any sort? I have no answer. Each must carry the question that perplexes to the Light of the World. To what purpose is the Spirit of God promised to them that ask it, if not to help them order their way aright?

One thing is plain—that we must love the strife-maker; another is nearly as plain—that, if we do not love him, we must leave him alone; for without love there can be no peacemaking, and words will but occasion more strife. To be kind neither hurts nor compromises. Kindness has many phases, and the fitting form of it may avoid offense, and must avoid untruth.

We must not fear what man can do to us, but commit our way to the Father of the Family. We must be nowise anxious to defend ourselves; and if not ourselves because God is our defense, then why our friends? Is He not their defense as much as ours?

Whatever our relation, then, with any peace-breaker, our mercy must ever be within call; and it may help us against an indignation too strong to be pure, to remember that when any man is reviled for righteousness' sake, then is he blessed.

THE REWARD
OF OBEDIENCE

"Blessed are the merciful, for they shall
obtain mercy. Blessed are
those who are persecuted for righteousness'
sake, for theirs is the
kingdom of heaven. Blessed are you when men
revile you and persecute you
and utter all kinds of evil against you
falsely on my account. Rejoice
and be glad, for your reward is great in heaven,
for so men persecuted the
prophets who were before you."
Matthew 5:7, 10-12.

Mercy cannot get in where mercy goes not out. The out-going makes way for the incoming. God takes the part of humanity against the man. The man must treat men as he would have God treat him. "If you forgive men their tresspasses, your heavenly Father also will forgive you; but if you do not forgive men their trespasses, neither will your Father forgive your trespasses." And in the prophecy of the judgment of the Son of Man, He represents Himself as saying, "As you did it to one of the least of these my brethren, you did it to me."

But the demand for mercy is far from being for the sake only of the man who needs his neighbor's mercy; it is greatly more for the sake of the man who must show the mercy. It is a small thing to a man whether or not his neighbor be merciful to him; it is life or death to him whether or not he be merciful to his neighbor. The greatest mercy that can be shown to a man is to make him merciful; therefore, if he will not be merciful, the mercy of God must compel him thereto.

In the parable of the king taking account of his servants, he delivers the unmerciful debtor to the tormentors, "till he should pay all that was due unto him." The king had forgiven his debtor, but as the debtor refuses to pass on the forgiveness to his neighbor—the only way to make a return in kind—the king withdraws his forgiveness. If we forgive not men their trespasses, our trespasses remain. For how can God in any sense forgive, remit, or send away the sin which a man insists on retaining?

Unmerciful, we must be given up to the tormentors until we learn to be merciful. God is merciful: we must be merciful. There is no blessedness except in being such as God; it would be altogether unmerciful to leave us unmerciful. The reward of the merciful is, that by their mercy they are rendered capable of receiving the mercy of God—yea, God Himself, who is Mercy.

That men may be drawn to taste and see and understand, the Lord associates reward with righteousness. The Lord would have men love righteousness, but how are they to love it without being acquainted with it? How are they to go on loving it without a growing knowledge of it? To draw them toward it that they may begin to know it, and to encourage them when assailed by the disappointments that accompany endeavor, He tells them simply a truth concerning it—that in the doing of it there is great reward.

The Nature of the Reward

The nature indeed of the Lord's promised rewards is hardly to be mistaken; yet the foolish remarks one sometimes hears make me wish to point out that neither is the Lord proclaiming an ethical system, nor does He make the blunder of representing as righteousness the doing of a good thing because of some advantage to be thereby gained. When He promises, He only states some fact that will encourage His disciples—that is, all who learn of Him —to meet the difficulties in the way of doing right and so learning righteousness, His object being to make men righteous, not to teach them philosophy.

It is the part of the enemy of righteousness to increase the difficulties in the way of becoming righteous, and to diminish those in the way of seeming righteous. Jesus desires no righteousness for the pride of being righteous, any more than for advantage to be gained by it; therefore, while requiring such purity as the man, beforehand, is unable to imagine, He gives him all the encouragement He can. He will not enhance his victory by difficulties—of them there are enough—but by completeness. He will not demand the loftiest motives in the yet far from loftiest soul: to those the soul must grow. He will hearten the child with promises, and fulfill them to the contentment of the man.

Men cannot be righteous without love; to love a righteous man is the best, the only way to learn righteousness: the Lord gives us Himself to love, and promises His closest friendship to them that overcome.

God's rewards are always in kind. "I am your Father; be my children, and I will be your Father." Every obedience is the opening of another door into the boundless universe of life. So long as the constitution of that universe remains, so long as the world continues to be made by God, righteousness can never fail of perfect reward. Before it could be otherwise, the government must have passed into other hands.

To be made greater than one's fellows is the offered reward of hell, and involves no greatness; to be made greater than one's self is the divine reward, and involves a real greatness. A man might be set above all his fellows, to be but so much less than he was before; a man cannot be raised a hair's-breadth above himself without rising nearer to God. The reward itself, then, is righteousness; and the man who was righteous for the sake of such reward, knowing what it was, would be righteous for the sake of righteousness—which yet, however, would not be perfection.

The reward of mercy is not often of this world; the merciful do not often receive mercy in return from their fellows; perhaps they do not often receive much gratitude. None the less, being the children of their Father in heaven, will they go on to show mercy, even to their enemies. They must give like God, and like God be blessed in giving.

There is a mercy that lies in the endeavor to share with others the best things God has given: they who do so will be persecuted and reviled and slandered, as well as thanked and loved and befriended. The Lord not only promises the greatest possible reward; He tells His disciples the worst they have to expect. He not only shows them the fair countries to which they are bound; He tells them the truth of the rough weather and the hardships of the way. He will not have them choose in ignorance. At the same time He strengthens them to meet coming difficulty by instructing them in its real nature.

All this is part of His preparation of them for His work, for taking His yoke upon them, and becoming fellow-laborers with Him in His Father's vineyard. They must not imagine, because they are the servants of His Father, that therefore they shall find their work easy; they shall only find the reward great.

9
THE YOKE OF JESUS

"At that time Jesus declared, 'I thank thee,
Father, Lord of heaven
and earth, that thou hast hidden these
things from the wise and understanding
and revealed them to babes;
yea, Father, for such was thy gracious will.
All things have been delivered
to me by my Father; and no one knows the
Son except the Father, and
no one knows the Father except the Son
and any one to whom the Son
chooses to reveal him. Come to me, all
who labor and are heavy laden,
and I will give you rest. Take my yoke upon you,
and learn from me; for I am
gentle and lowly in heart, and you will
find rest for your souls. For my
yoke is easy, and my burden is light.' "
Matthew 11:25-30 (cf. Matt. 18:10, 14; Luke 15:10).

The Lord makes no complaint against the wise and prudent [King James Version]; He but recognizes that they are not those to whom His Father reveals His best things, for which fact, and the reasons of it, He thanks or praises His Father. "I bless thy will: I see that thou art right: I am of one mind with thee": something of each of these phases of meaning seems to belong to the Greek word.

"But why not reveal true things first to the wise? Are they not the fittest to receive them?" Yes, if these things and their wisdom lie in the same region—not otherwise. No amount of knowledge or skill in physical science will make a man the fitter to argue a metaphysical question; and the wisdom of this world, meaning by the term, the philosophy of prudence, self-protection, precaution, specially unfits a man for receiving what the Father has to reveal: in proportion to our care about our own well-being is our incapability of understanding and welcoming the care of the Father.

The wise and the prudent, with all their energy of thought, could never see the things of the Father sufficiently to recognize them as true. Their sagacity labors in earthly things, and so fills their minds with their own questions and conclusions that they cannot see the eternal foundations God has laid in man, or the consequent necessities of their own nature. They are proud of finding out things, but the things they find out are all less than themselves. Because, however they have discovered them, they imagine such things the goal of the human intellect.

If they grant there may be things beyond those, they either count them beyond their reach, or declare themselves uninterested in them: for the wise and prudent they do not exist. They work only to gather by the senses, and deduce from what they have so gathered the prudential, the probable, the expedient, the protective. They never think of the essential, of what in itself must be. They are cautious, wary, discreet, judicious, circumspect, provident, temporizing.

They have no enthusiasm, and are shy of all forms of it—a clever, hard, thin people, who take *things* for the universe, and love of facts for love of truth. They know nothing deeper in man than mere surface mental facts and their relations. They do not perceive, or they turn away from any truth which the intellect cannot formulate. Zeal for God will never eat them up: why should it? He is not interesting to them: theology may be; to such men religion means theology.

How should the treasure of the Father be open to such? Even when they know their duty, they must take it to pieces, and consider the grounds of its claim before they will render it obedience. All those evil doctrines about God that work misery and madness have their origin in the brains of the wise and prudent, not in the hearts of the children.

These wise and prudent, careful to make the words of His messengers rime with their conclusions, interpret the great heart of God, not by their own hearts, but by their miserable intellects; and, postponing the obedience which alone can give power to the understanding, press upon men's minds their wretched interpretations of the will of the Father, instead of the doing of that will upon their hearts. They call their philosophy the truth of God, and say men must hold it, or stand outside. They are the slaves of the letter in all its weakness and imperfection—and will be until the spirit of the Word, the spirit of obedience, shall set them free.

The babes must beware lest the wise and prudent come between them and the Father. They must yield no claim to authority over their belief, made by man or community, by church any more than by synagogue. That alone is for them to believe which the Lord reveals to their souls as true; that alone is it possible for them to believe with what He counts belief. The divine object for which teacher or church exists is the persuasion of the individual heart to come to Jesus, the Spirit, to be taught what He alone can teach.

Terribly has His gospel suffered in the mouths of the wise and prudent: how would it be faring now, had its first messages been committed to persons of repute, instead of those simple fishermen? It would be nowhere, or, if anywhere, unrecognizable. From the first we should have had a system founded on a human interpretation of the divine gospel, instead of the gospel itself, which would have disappeared. As it is, we have had one dull, miserable human system after another usurping its place; but, thank God, the gospel remains!

Had the wise and prudent been the confidants of God, I repeat, the letter would at once have usurped the place of the spirit; the ministering slave would have been set over the household; a system of religion, with its rickety, malodorous plan of salvation, would not only have at once been put in the place of a living Christ, but would yet have held that place. The great Brother, the human God, the eternal Son, the living One, would have been as utterly hidden from the tearful eyes and aching hearts of the weary and heavy-laden as if He had never come from the deeps of love to call the children home out of the shadows of a self-haunted universe.

But the Father revealed the Father's things to His babes; the babes loved, and began to do them, therewith began to understand them, and went on growing in the knowledge of them and in the power of communicating them; while to the wise and prudent the deepest words of the most babe-like of them all, John Boanerges, even now appear but a finger-worn rosary of platitudes. The babe understands the wise and prudent, but is understood only by the babe.

Only Babes Can See

The Father, then, revealed His things to babes because the babes were His own little ones, uncorrupted by the wisdom or the care of this world, and therefore able to receive them. The others, though His children, had not begun to be like Him, therefore could not receive them. The Father's things could not have got anyhow into their minds without leaving all their value, all their spirit, outside the unchild-like place.

The babes are near enough whence they come to understand a little how things go in the presence of their Father in heaven, and thereby to interpret the words of the Son. As God is the one only real Father, so is it only to God that any one can be a perfect child.

Having thanked His Father that He has done after his own "good and acceptable and perfect will," He turns to His disciples, and tells them that He knows the Father, being His Son, and that He only can reveal the Father to the rest of His children.

It is almost as if His mention of the babes brought His thoughts back to Himself and His Father, between whom lay the secret of all life and all sending—yea, all loving. The relation of the Father and the Son contains the idea of the universe.

Jesus tells His disciples that His Father had no secrets from Him; that He knew the Father as the Father knew Him. The Son must know the Father; He only could know Him— and knowing, He could reveal Him; the Son could make the others, the imperfect children, know the Father, and so become such as He. All things were given unto Him by the Father, because He was the Son of the Father: for the same reason He could reveal the things of the Father to the child of the Father. The child-relation is the one eternal, ever-enduring, never-changing relation.

Note that, while the Lord here represents the knowledge His Father and He have each of the other as limited to themselves, the statement is one of fact only, not of design or intention: His presence in the world is for the removal of that limitation. The Father knows the Son, and sends Him to us that we may know Him; the Son knows the Father, and dies to reveal Him. The glory of God's mysteries is, that they are for His children to look into.

When the Lord took the little child in the presence of His disciples, and declared him His representative, He made him the representative of His Father also; but the eternal Child alone can reveal Him. To reveal is immeasurably more than to represent; it is to present to the eyes that know the true when they see it. Jesus represented God; the spirit of Jesus reveals God.

The represented God a man may refuse; many refused

the Lord; the revealed God no one can refuse; to see God and to love Him are one. He can be revealed only to the child; perfectly, to the pure child only. All the discipline of the world is to make men children, that God may be revealed to them.

No man, when first he comes to himself, can have any true knowledge of God; he can only have a desire after such knowledge. But while he does not know Him at all, he cannot become in his heart God's child; so the Father must draw nearer to him. He sends therefore His First-born, who does know Him, is exactly like Him, and can represent Him perfectly.

Drawn to Him, the children receive Him, and then He is able to reveal the Father to them. No wisdom of the wise can find out God; no words of the God-loving can reveal Him. The simplicity of the whole natural relation is too deep for the philosopher. The Son alone can reveal God; the child alone understand Him.

Taking His Yoke

Having spoken to His Father first, and now to His disciples, the Lord turns to the whole world, and lets His heart overflow. St. Matthew alone has saved for us the eternal cry: "Come to me, all who labor and are heavy laden, and I will give you rest." He does not here call those who want to know the Father; His cry goes far beyond them; it reaches to the ends of the earth. He calls those who are weary; those who do not know that ignorance of the Father is the cause of all their labor and the heaviness of their burden. "Come to me," He says, "and I will give you rest."

I will turn His argument a little: "I have rest because I know the Father. Be meek and lowly of heart toward Him as I am; let Him lay His yoke upon you as He lays it on me. I do His will, not my own. Take on you the yoke that I wear; be His child like me; become a babe to whom He can reveal His wonders. Then shall you too find rest to your souls; you shall have the same peace I have; you will be weary and heavy laden no more. I find my yoke easy, my burden light."

The best of the good wine remains; I have kept it to the last. A friend pointed out to me that the Master does not mean we must take on us a yoke like His; we must take on us the very yoke He is carrying.

Dante, describing how, on the first terrace of Purgatory, he walked stooping, to be on a level with Oderisi, who went bowed to the ground by the ponderous burden of the pride he had cherished on earth, says, "I went walking with this heavy-laden soul, just as oxen walk in the yoke": this picture almost always comes to me with the words of the Lord, "Take my yoke upon you, and learn of me." Their intent is, "Take the other end of my yoke, doing as I do, being as I am."

Think of it a moment: to walk in the same yoke with the Son of Man, doing the same labor with Him, and having the same feeling common to Him and us! This, and nothing else, is offered the man who would have rest to his soul; is required of the man who would know the Father; is by the Lord pressed upon him to whom He would give the same peace which pervades and sustains His own eternal heart.

But a yoke is for drawing: what load is it the Lord is drawing? Wherewith is the cart laden which He would have us help Him draw? With what but the will of the eternal, the perfect Father? How should the Father honor the Son, but by giving Him His will to embody in deed? Specially in drawing this load must His yoke-fellow share. How to draw it, he must learn of Him who draws by his side.

Whoever, in the commonest duties that fall to him, does as the Father would have him do, bears his yoke along with Jesus. Bearing the same yoke with Jesus, the man learns to walk step for step with Him drawing, drawing the cart laden with the will of the Father of both, and rejoicing with the joy of Jesus.

The glory of existence is to take up its burden, and exist

for Existence eternal and supreme—for the Father who does His divine and perfect best to impart His glad life to us, making us sharers of that nature which is bliss, and that labor which is peace. He lives for us; we must live for Him. The little ones must take their full share in the great Father's work: His work is the business of the family.

He on whom lay the other half of the burden of God, the weight of His creation to redeem, says, "The yoke I bear is easy; the burden I draw is light"; and this He said, knowing the death He was to die. The yoke did not gall His neck, the burden did not overstrain His sinews, neither did the goal on Calvary fright Him from the straight way thither. He had the will of the Father to work out, and that will was His strength as well as His joy. He had the same will as His Father. To Him the one thing worth living for was the share the love of his Father gave Him in His work. He loved His Father even to the death of the cross, and eternally beyond it.

When we give ourselves up to the Father as the Son gave Himself, we shall not only find our yoke easy and our burden light, but that they communicate ease and lightness; not only will they not make us weary, but they will give us rest from all other weariness. Let us not waste a moment in asking how this can be; the only way to know that is to take the yoke on us. That rest is a secret for every heart to know, for never a tongue to tell. Only by having it can we know it.

If it seem impossible to take the yoke on us, let us attempt the impossible; let us lay hold of the yoke, and bow our heads, and try to get our necks under it. Giving our Father the opportunity, He will help and not fail us. He is helping us every moment, when least we think we need His help; when most we think we do, then may we most boldly, as most earnestly we must, cry for it.

What or how much His creatures can do or bear, God only understands; but when most it seems impossible to do or bear, we must be most confident that He will neither demand too much, nor fail with the vital creator-help. That help will be there when wanted—that is, the moment it can be help. To be able beforehand to imagine ourselves doing or bearing, we have neither claim nor need.

It is vain to think that any weariness, however caused, any burden, however slight, may be got rid of otherwise than by bowing the neck to the yoke of the Father's will. There can be no other rest for heart and soul that He has created. From every burden, from every anxiety, from all dread of shame or loss, even loss of love itself, that yoke will set us free.

Those who come at the call of the Lord, and take the rest He offers them, learning of Him, and bearing the yoke of the Father, are the salt of the earth, the light of the world.

10

THE SALT AND
THE LIGHT OF THE WORLD

" 'You are the salt of the earth; but if
salt has lost its taste, how shall its saltness be restored?
It is no longer good
for anything except to be thrown out and trodden
under foot by men. You are
the light of the world. A city set on a
hill cannot be hid. Nor do men
light a lamp and put it under a bushel,
but on a stand, and it gives light to all in the house. Let your light
so shine before men, that they
may see your good works and give glory to
your Father who is in heaven.' "
Matthew 5:13-16.

... The Lord does not hesitate to call His few humble disciples the salt of the earth; and every century since has borne
witness that such indeed they were—that He spoke of them
but the simple fact. Where would the world be now but for
their salt and their light!

The world that knows neither their salt nor their light
may imagine itself now at least greatly retarded by the
long-drawn survival of their influences; but such as have
chosen aspiration and not ambition will cry, But for those
men, whither should we at this moment be bound?

Their Master set them to be salt against corruption, and light against darkness; and our souls answer and say, Lord, they have been the salt, they have been the light of the world.

No sooner had He used the symbol of the salt, than the Lord proceeds to supplement its incompleteness. They were salt which must remember that it is salt; which must live salt, and choose salt, and be salt. For the whole worth of salt lies in its being salt; and all the saltness of the moral salt lies in the will to be salt. To lose its saltness, then, is to cease to exist, save as a vile thing whose very being is un-justifiable. What is to be done with saltless salt? with such as would teach religion and know not God?

Having thus carried the figure as far as it will serve Him, the Master changes it for another, which He can carry fur-ther. For salt only preserves from growing bad; it does not cause anything to grow better. His disciples are the salt of the world, but they are more. Therefore, having warned the human salt to look to itself that it be indeed salt, He pro-ceeds: "You are the light of the world, a city, a candle," and so resumes His former path of persuasion and enforcement: "It is so; therefore make it so. You are the salt of the earth; therefore be salt. You are the light of the world; therefore shine. You are a city; be seen upon your hill. You are the Lord's candles; let no bushels cover you. Let your light shine." Every disciple of the Lord must be a preacher of righteousness.

Cities are the best lighted portions of the world; and per-haps the Lord meant, "You are a live city; therefore light up your city." Some connection of the city with light seems probably in His thought, seeing the allusion to the city on the hill comes in the midst of what He says about light in relation to His disciples as the light of the world. Anyhow the city is the best circle in which, and the best center from which, to diffuse moral light. A man brooding in the desert may find the very light of light, but he must go to the city to let it shine.

From the general idea of light, however associated with the city as visible to all the country around, the Lord turns at once, in this probably fragmentary representation of His words, to the homelier, the more individual and personally applicable figure of the lamp: "Nor do men light a lamp and put it under a bushel, but on a stand, and it gives light to all in the house."

Lighted for God

Here let us meditate a moment. For what is a lamp or a man lighted? For them that need light, therefore for all. A candle is not lighted for itself; neither is a man. The light that serves self only is no true light; its one virtue is that it will soon go out. The bushel needs to be lighted, but not by being put over the lamp. The man's own soul needs to be lighted, but light for itself only, light covered by the bushel, is darkness whether to soul or bushel.

Light unshared is darkness. To be light indeed, it must shine out. It is of the very essence of light, that it is for others. The thing is true of the spiritual as of the physical light—of the truth as of its type.

The lights of the world are live lights. The lamp that the Lord kindles is a lamp that can will to shine, a soul that must shine. Its true relation to the spirits around it—to God and its fellows—is its light. Then only does it fully shine, when its love, which is its light, shows it to all the souls within its scope, and all those souls to each other, and so does its part to bring all together toward one. In the darkness each soul is alone; in the light the souls are a family.

Men do not light a lamp to kill with a bushel, but to set it on a stand, that it may give light to all that are in the house. The Lord seems to say, "So have I lighted you, not that you may shine for yourselves, but that you may give light unto all. I have set you like a city on a hill, that the whole earth may see and share in your light. Shine therefore; so shine before men, that they may see your good things and glorify your Father for the light with which He has lighted you.

Take heed to your light that it be such, that it so shine, that in you men may see the Father—may see your works so good, so plainly His, that they recognize His presence in you, and thank Him for you."

There was the danger always of the shadow of the self-bushel clouding the lamp the Father had lighted; and the moment they ceased to show the Father, the light that was in them was darkness. God alone is the light, and our light is the shining of His will in our lives. If our light shine at all, it must be, it can be only in showing the Father; nothing is light that does not bear Him witness.

The man that sees the glory of God would turn sick at the thought of glorifying his own self, whose one only possible glory is to shine with the glory of God. When a man tries to shine from the self that is not one with God and filled with His light, he is but making ready for his own gathering contempt. The man who, like his Lord, seeks not his own, but the will of Him who sent him, he alone shines. He who would shine in the praises of men will, sooner or later, find himself but a Gideon's pitcher left broken on the field.

Let us bestir ourselves then, to keep this word of the Lord; and to this end inquire how we are to let our light shine.

Maintaining One's Light

To the man who does not try to order his thoughts and feelings and judgments after the will of the Father, I have nothing to say; he can have no light to let shine. For to let our light shine is to see that in every, even the smallest thing, our lives and actions correspond to what we know of God; that, as the true children of our Father in heaven, we do everything as He would have us do it.

Need I say that to let our light shine is to be just, honorable, true, courteous, more careful over the claim of our neighbor than our own, as knowing ourselves in danger of overlooking it, and not bound to insist on every claim of our own? The man who takes no count of what is fair, friendly, pure, unselfish, lovely, gracious—where is his claim to Christianity? What saves his claim from being merest mockery?

The outshining of any human light must be obedience to truth recognized as such; our first show of light as the Lord's disciples must be in doing the things He tells us. Naturally thus we declare Him our Master, the ruler of our conduct, the enlightener of our souls; and while in the doing of His will a man is learning the loveliness of right-eousness, he can hardly fail to let some light shine across the dust of his failures, the exhalations from his faults. Thus will His disciples shine as lights in the world, holding forth the Word of life.

To shine, we must keep in His light, sunning our souls in it by thinking of what He said and did, and would have us think and do. So shall we drink the light like some dia-monds, keep it, and shine in the dark. Doing His will, men will see in us that we count the world His, hold that His will and not ours must be done in it. Our very faces will then shine with the hope of seeing Him, and being taken home where He is. Only let us remember that trying to look what we ought to be is the beginning of hypocrisy.

If we do indeed expect better things to come, we must let our hope appear. A Christian who looks gloomy at the men-tion of death, still more, one who talks of his friends as if he had lost them, turns the bushel of his little-faith over the lamp of the Lord's light. Death is but our visible horizon, and our look ought always to be focused beyond it. We should never talk as if death were the end of anything.

To let our light shine, we must take care that we have no respect for riches: if we have none, there is no fear of our showing any. To treat the poor man with less attention or cordiality than the rich is to show ourselves the servants of Mammon. In like manner we must lay no value on the praise of men, or in any way seek it. We must honor no man because of intellect, fame, or success. We must not shrink, in fear of the judgment of men, from doing openly what we hold right; or at all acknowledge as a law-giver what calls itself Society, or harbor the least anxiety for its approval.

In business, the custom of the trade must be understood by both contracting parties, else it can have no place, either as law or excuse, with the disciple of Jesus. The man to whom business is one thing and religion another is not a disciple. If he refuses to harmonize them by making his business religion, he has already chosen Mammon; if he thinks not to settle the question, it is settled. The most futile of all human endeavors is, to serve God and Mammon. The man who makes the endeavor betrays his Master in the temple and kisses Him in the garden; takes advantage of Him in the shop, and offers Him "divine service" on Sunday. His very church-going is but a further service of Mammon.

But let us waste no strength in despising such men; let us rather turn the light upon ourselves: are we not in some way denying Him? Is our light bearing witness? Is it shining before men so that they glorify God for it? If it does not shine, it is darkness.

But if all our light shine out, and none of our darkness, shall we not be in utmost danger of hypocrisy? Yes, if we but hide our darkness, and do not strive to slay it with our light: what way have we to show it, while struggling to destroy it? Only when we cherish evil is there hypocrisy in hiding it. A man who is honestly fighting it and showing it no quarter is already conqueror in Christ, or will soon be—and more than innocent.

But our good feelings, those that make for righteousness and unity, we ought to let shine; they claim to commune with the light in others. Many parents hold words unsaid which would lift hundredweights from the hearts of their children, make them leap for joy. A stern father and a silent mother make mournful, or, which is far wrose, hard children. Need I add that, if any one, having the injunction to let his light shine, makes himself shine instead, it is because the light is not in him.

Shining Freely

"Let your light shine," says the Lord: if I have none, the call cannot apply to me; but I must bethink me, lest, in the night I am cherishing about me, the Lord come upon me like a thief. There may be those, however, and I think they are numerous, who, having some, or imagining they have much light, yet have not enough to know the duty of letting it shine on their neighbors.

Friend, let the joy of thy hope stream forth upon thy neighbors. Fold them round in that which maketh thyself glad. Let thy nature grow more expansive and communicative. Look like the man thou art—a man who knows something very good. Thou believest thyself on the way to the heart of things: walk so, shine so, that all that see thee shall want to go with thee.

What light issues from such as make their faces long at the very name of death, and look and speak as if it were the end of all things and the worst of evils? Jesus told His men not to fear death; told them His friends should go to be with Him; told them they should live in the house of His Father and their Father; and since then He has risen Himself from the tomb, and gone to prepare a place for them: who, what are these miserable refusers of comfort? Not Christians, surely!

Oh, yes, they are Christians! "They are gone," they say, "to be forever with the Lord"; then they weep and lament, and seem more afraid of starting to join them than of aught else under the sun. To the last attainable moment, they cling to what they call life. They are children—were there ever any other such children?—who hang crying to the skirts of their mother, and will not be lifted to her bosom.

They are not of Paul's mind: to be with Him is not better! They worship their physician; and their prayer to the God of their life is to spare them from more life. What sort of Christians are they? Where shine their light? Alas for thee, poor world, hadst thou no better lights than these!

You who have light, show yourselves the sons and daughters of Light, of God, of Hope—the heirs of a great completeness. Freely let your light shine.

11
THE RIGHT HAND
AND THE LEFT

" 'Beware of practicing your piety before
men in order to be seen
by them; for then you will have no reward from
your Father who is in heaven.
But when you give alms, do not let your
left hand know what your
right hand is doing, so that your alms may be
in secret; and your Father who
sees in secret will reward you.' "
Matthew 6:1, 3, 4.

Let your light out freely, that men may see it, but not that men may see you. If I do anything [in order] that I may be seen as the doer, that I may be praised of men, that I may gain repute of others; be the thing itself ever so good, I may look to men for my reward, for there is none for me with the Father.

If I do it that the light may shine, and that men may know *the* Light, the Father of lights, I do well; but if I do it that I may be seen shining, that the light may be noted as emanating from me and not from another, then am I of those that seek glory of men, and worship Satan; the light that through me may possibly illuminate others, will, in me and for me, be darkness.

The injunction, however, is not to hide what you do from others, but to hide it from yourself. The Master would have you not plume yourself upon it, not cherish the thought that you have done it, or confer with yourself in satisfaction over it. You must not count it to your praise. A man must not desire to be satisfied with himself. His right hand must not seek the praise of his left hand. His doing must not invite his after-thinking. The right hand must let the thing done go, as a thing done with.

When we have done all, we are unprofitable servants. Our very best is but decent. What more could it be? Why then think of it as anything more? What things could we or any one do, worthy of being brooded over as possessions? Good to do, they were; bad to pride ourselves upon, they are. Why should a man meditate with satisfaction on having denied himself some selfish indulgence, any more than on having washed his hands?

Even if our supposed merit were of the positive order, and we did every duty perfectly, the moment we began to pride ourselves upon the fact we should drop into a hell of worthlessness. What are we for but to do our duty? We must do it, and think nothing of ourselves for that, neither care what men think of us for anything. With the praise or blame of men we have nought to do.

The Nature of Rewards
But there are some who, if the notion of reward is not naturally a trouble to them, yet have come to feel it such, because of the words of certain objectors who think to take a higher stand than the Christian, saying the idea of reward for doing right is a low, an unworthy idea. Now, verily, it would be a low thing for any child to do his father's will in the hope that his father would reward him for it; but it is quite another thing for a father whose child endeavors to please him, to let him know that he recognizes his childness toward him, and will be a fatherly good to him.

What kind of a father were the man who, because there

could be no merit or desert in doing well, would not give his child a smile or a pleased word when he saw him trying his best? Would not such acknowledgment from the father be the natural correlate of the child's behavior? and what would the father's smile be but the perfect reward of the child? Suppose the father to love the child so that he wants to give him everything, but dares not until his character is developed: must he not be glad, and show his gladness, at every shade of a progress that will at length set him free to throne his son over all that he has?

If you say, "No one ought to do right for the sake of reward," I go further and say, "No man *can* do right for the sake of reward. A man may do a thing indifferent, he may do a thing wrong, for the sake of reward; but a thing in itself right, done for reward, would, in the very doing, cease to be right." At the same time, if a man does right, he cannot escape being rewarded for it; and to refuse the reward would be to refuse life, and foil the creative love.

The whole question is of the kind of reward expected. What first reward for doing well may I look for? To grow purer in heart, and stronger in the hope of at length seeing God. If a man be not after this fashion rewarded, he must perish. As to happiness or any lower rewards that naturally follow the first—is God to destroy the law of His universe, the divine sequence of cause and effect in order to say: "You must do well, but you shall gain no good by it; you must lead a dull, joyless existence to all eternity, that lack of delight may show you pure"? Could Love create with such end in view?

A righteousness that created misery in order to uphold itself would be a righteousness that was unrighteous. God will die for righteousness, but never create for a joyless righteousness. To call into being the necessarily and hopelessly incomplete would be to wrong creation in its very essence. To create for the knowledge of Himself, and then not give Himself, would be injustice even to cruelty; and if God give Himself, what other reward—there can be no *further*—

is not included, seeing He is Life and all her children—the All in all?

To object to Christianity as selfish is utter foolishness; Christianity alone gives any hope of deliverance from self-ishness. Is it selfish to desire love? Is it selfish to hope for purity and the sight of God? What better can we do for our neighbor than to become altogether righteous toward him? Will he not be the nearer sharing in the exceeding great reward of a return to the divine idea?

Merit before God

It seems to me that the only merit that could live before God is the merit of Jesus—who of Himself, at once, unim-plored, laid Himself aside, and turned to the Father, refus-ing His life save in the Father. Like God, of Himself He chose righteousness, and so merited to sit on the throne of God. In the same spirit He gave himself afterward to His Father's children, and merited the power to transfuse the life-redeeming energy of His spirit into theirs: made per-fect, He became the author of eternal salvation unto all them that obey Him. But it is a word of little daring, that Jesus had no thought of merit in what He did—that He saw only what He had to be, what He must do.

I suspect the notion of merit belongs to a low develop-ment, and the higher a man rises, the less will he find it worth a thought. Perhaps we shall come to see that it owes what being it has to man, that it is a thing thinkable only by man. I suspect it is not a thought of the eternal mind, and has in itself no existence, being to God merely a thing thought by man.

> For merit lives from man to man,
> And not from man, O Lord, to thee.

The man, then, who does right, and seeks no praise from men, while he merits nothing, shall be rewarded by his Father, and his reward will be right precious to him.

We must let our light shine, make our faith, our hope, our love, manifest—that men may praise, not us for shining, but the Father for creating the light. No man with faith, hope, love, alive in his soul, could make the divine possessions a show to gain for himself the admiration of men: not the less must they appear in our words, in our looks, in our carriage—above all, in honorable, unselfish hospitable, helpful deeds.

Our light must shine in cheerfulness, in joy, yea, where a man has the gift, in merriment; in freedom from care save for one another, in interest in the things of others, in fearlessness and tenderness; in courtesy and graciousness. In our anger and indignation, specially, must our light shine. But we must give no quarter to the most shadowy thought of how this or that will look. From the faintest thought of the praise of men, we must turn away.

No man can be the disciple of Christ and desire fame. To desire fame is ignoble; it is a beggarly greed. In the noble mind, it is the more of an infirmity. There is no aspiration in it—nothing but ambition. It is simply selfishness that would be proud if it could. Fame is the applause of the many, and the judgment of the many is foolish; therefore the greater the fame, the more is the foolishness that swells it, and the worse is the foolishness that longs after it.

Aspiration is the sole escape from ambition. He who aspires—that is, does his endeavor to rise above himself —neither lusts to be higher than his neighbor, nor seeks to mount in his opinion. What light there is in him shines the more that he does nothing to be seen of men. He stands in the mist between the gulf and the glory, and looks upward. He loves not his own soul, but longs to be clean.

12
THE HOPE OF
THE UNIVERSE

*"For the creation waits with eager longing
for the revealing of the sons of God."*
Romans 8:19.

Let us try, through these words, to get at the idea in St.
Paul's mind for which they stand, and have so long stood.
It can be no worthless idea they represent—no mere plati-
tude, which a man, failing to understand it at once, may
without loss leave behind him. The words mean something
which Paul believes vitally associated with the life and
death of his Master.

He had seen Jesus with his bodily eyes, I think, but he
had not seen Him with those alone; he had seen and saw
Him with the real eyes, the eyes that do not see except they
understand, and the sight of Him had uplifted his whole
nature—first his pure will for righteousness, and then his
hoping imagination; and out of these, in the knowledge of
Jesus, he spoke.

The Scope of "Creation"
First then, what does Paul, the slave of Christ, intend by
"the creature" or "the creation"? If he means the visible
world, he did not surely, and without saying so, mean to

exclude the noblest part of it—the sentient! If he did, it is doubly strange that he should immediately attribute not merely sense, but conscious sense, to that part, the insentient, namely, which remained. If you say he does so but by a figure of speech, I answer that a figure that meant less than it said—and how much less would not this?—would be one altogether unworthy of the Lord's messenger.

Take another part of the same utterance: "We know that the whole creation has been groaning in travail together until now": is it now manifest that to interpret such words as referring to the mere imperfections of the insensate material world would be to make of the phrase a worthless hyperbole? I am inclined to believe the apostle regarded the whole visible creation as, in far differing degrees of consciousness, a live outcome from the heart of the living one, who is all and in all: such view, at the same time, I do not care to insist upon; I only care to argue that the word *creature* or *creation* must include everything in creation that has sentient life.

That I should in the class include a greater number of phenomena than a reader may be prepared to admit, will nowise affect the force of what I have to say, seeing my point is simply this: that in the term *creation* Paul comprises all creatures capable of suffering; the condition of which sentient, therefore superior portion, gives him occasion to speak of the whole creation as suffering in the process of its divine evolution or development, groaning and travailing as in the pangs of giving birth to a better self, a nobler world.

It is not necessary to the idea that the creation should know what it is groaning after, or wherein the higher condition constituting its deliverance must consist. The human race groans for deliverance: how much does the race know that its redemption lies in becoming one with the Father, and partaking of His glory? Here and there one of the race knows it—which is indeed a pledge for the race— but the race cannot be said to know its own lack, or to have even a far-off notion of what alone can stay its groaning.

In like manner the whole creation is groaning after an unforeseen yet essential birth—groans with the necessity of being freed from a state that is but a transitional and not a true one, from a condition that nowise answers to the intent in which existence began. In both the lower creation and the higher, this same groaning of the fettered idea after a freer life seems the first enforced decree of a holy fate, and itself the first movement of the hampered thing toward the liberty of another birth.

The God of the Sparrow

To believe that God made many of the lower creatures merely for prey, or to be the slaves of a slave, and writhe under the tyrannies of a cruel master who will not serve his own master; that He created and is creating an endless succession of them to reap little or no good of life but its cessation—a doctrine held by some, and practically accepted by multitudes—is to believe in a God who, so far as one portion at least of His creation is concerned, is a demon.

But a creative demon is an absurdity; and were such a creator possible, he would not be God, but must one day be found and destroyed by the real God. Not the less the fact remains, that miserable suffering abounds among them, and that, even supposing God did not foresee how creation would turn out for them, the thing lies at His door. He has besides made them so far dumb that they cannot move the hearts of the oppressors into whose hands He has given them, telling how hard they find the world, how sore their life in it. The apostle takes up their case, and gives us material for an answer to such as blame God for their sad condition.

What many men call their beliefs are but the prejudices they happen to have picked up. But there are not a few who would be indignant at having their belief in God questioned, who yet seem greatly to fear imagining Him better than He is. "You see the plain facts of the case," they say.

"There is no questioning them. What can be done for the poor things—except, indeed, you take the absurd notion into your head, that they too have a life beyond the grave?"

Why should such a notion seem to you absurd? I answer. The teachers of the nation have unwittingly, it seems to me through unbelief, wronged the animals deeply by their silence against the thoughtless popular presumption that they have no hereafter, thus leaving them deprived of a great advantage to their position among men. But I suppose they too have taken it for granted that the Preserver of man and beast never had a thought of keeping one beast alive beyond a certain time; in which case heartless men might well argue He did not care how they wronged them, for He meant them no redress. Their immortality is no new faith with me, but as old as my childhood.

Do you believe in immortality for yourself? I would ask any reader who is not in sympathy with my hope for the animals. If not, I have no argument with you. But if you do, why not believe in it for them? Are these not worth making immortal? How, then, were they worth calling out of the depth of no-being?

It is a greater deed, to make be that which was not, then to seal it with an infinite immortality: did God do that which was not worth doing? What He thought worth making, you think not worth continuing made! You would have Him go on forever creating new things with one hand, and annihilating those He had made with the other—for I presume you would not prefer the earth to be without animals. If it were harder for God to make the former go on living than to send forth new, then His creatures were no better than the toys which a child makes, and destroys as he makes them.

For what good, for what divine purpose is the Maker of the sparrow present at its death, if He does not care what becomes of it? What is He there for, I repeat, if He have no care that it go well with His bird in its dying, that it be neither comfortless nor lost in the abyss? If His presence be no good to the sparrow, are you very sure what good it will be to you when your hour comes? Believe it is not by a little only that the heart of the universe is tenderer, more loving, more just and fair, than yours or mine.

If you did not believe you were yourself to outlive death, I could not blame you for thinking all was over with the sparrow; but to believe in immortality for yourself, and not care to believe in it for the sparrow, would be simply hardhearted and selfish. If it would make you happy to think there was life beyond death for the sparrow as well as for yourself, I would gladly help you at least to hope that there may be.

I know of no reason why I should not look for the animals to rise again, in the same sense in which I hope myself to rise again—which is, to reappear, clothed with another and better form of life than before. If the Father will raise His children, why should He not also raise those whom He has taught His little ones to love?

Love is the one bond of the universe, the heart of God, the life of His children: if animals can be loved, they are lovable; if they can love, they are yet more plainly lovable: love is eternal; how then should its object perish? Must the love live on forever without its object? or, worse still, must the love die with its object, and be eternal no more than it?

Is not our love to the animals a precious variety of love? And if God gave the creatures to us, that a new phase of love might be born in us toward another kind of life from the same fountain, why should the new life be more perishing than the new love?

Can you imagine that, if, hereafter, one of God's little ones were to ask Him to give again one of the earth's old loves—kitten, or pony, or squirrel, or dog, which He had taken from him, the Father would say no? If the thing was so good that God made it for and gave it to the child at first who never asked for it, why should He not give it again to the child who prays for it because the Father had made him love it? What a child may ask for, the Father will keep ready.

Facing a Difficulty

That there are difficulties in the way of believing thus, I grant; that there are impossibilities, I deny. Perhaps the first difficulty that occurs is, the many forms of life which we cannot desire again to see. But while we would gladly keep the perfected forms of the higher animals, we may hope that those of many other kinds are as transitory as their bodies, belonging but to a stage of development. All animal forms tend to higher: why should not the individual, as well as the race, pass through stages of ascent?

The suggestion may appear very ridiculous, and no doubt lends itself to humorous comment; but what if it should be true! what if the amused reader should himself be getting ready to follow the remanded ancestor? Upon it, however, I do not care to spend thought or time, least of all argument.

What I care to press is the question—If we believe in the progress of creation as hitherto manifested, also in the marvelous changes of form that take place in every individual of certain classes, why should there be any difficulty in hoping that old lives may reappear in new forms? The typal soul reappears in higher formal type; why may not also the individual soul reappear in higher form?

Multitudes evidently count it safest to hold by a dull scheme of things.... Those that hope little cannot grow much. To them the very glory of God must be a small thing, for their hope of it is so small as not to be worth rejoicing in. That He is a faithful creator means nothing to them for far the larger portion of the creatures He has made. Truly their notion of faithfulness is poor enough; how, then, can their faith be strong?

In the very nature of divine things, the commonplace must be false. The stupid, self-satisfied soul, which cannot know its own stupidity, and will not trouble itself either to understand or to imagine, is the farthest behind of all the backward children in God's nursery.

As I say, then, I know no cause of reasonable difficulty

in regard to the continued existence of the lower animals, except the present nature of some of them. But what Christian will dare to say that God does not care about them?—and He knows them as we cannot know them. Great are all His results; small are all His beginnings.

That we have to send many of His creatures out of this phase of their life because of their hurtfulness in this phase of ours, is to me no stumbling block. The very fact that this has always had to be done, the long-protracted combat of the race with such, and the constantly repeated though not invariable victory of the man, has had an essential and incalculable share in the development of humanity, which is the rendering of man capable of knowing God; and when their part to that end is no longer necessary, changed conditions may speedily so operate that the wolf shall dwell with the lamb, and the leopard lie down with the kid. The difficulty may go for nothing in view of the forces of that future with which this loving speculation concerns itself.

Delivered from Corruption

I would now lead my companion a little closer to what the apostle says in the nineteenth verse; to come closer, if we may, to the idea that burned in his heart when he wrote what we call the eighth chapter of his epistle to the Romans. Oh, how far ahead he seems, in his hope for the creation, of the footsore and halting brigade of Christians at present crossing the world! He knew Christ, and could therefore look into the will of his Father.

"For the creation waits with eager longing for the revealing of the sons of God."

At the head of one of his poems, Henry Vaughan has this Latin translation of the verse: I do not know whether he found or made it, but it is closer to its [true] sense than ours: "For the things created, watching with head thrust out, await the revelation of the sons of God."

Why? Because God has subjected the creation to vanity [RSV: futility], in the hope that the creation itself shall be delivered from the bondage of corruption into the glorious liberty of the children of God. For this double deliverance— from corruption and the consequent subjection to vanity, the creation is eagerly watching.

The bondage of corruption God encounters and counteracts by subjection to vanity. Corruption is the breaking up of the essential idea; the falling away from the original indwelling . . . thought. It is met by the suffering which itself causes. That suffering is for redemption, for deliverance. It is the life in the corrupting thing that makes the suffering possible; it is the live part, not the corrupted part, that suffers; it is the redeemable, not the doomed thing, that is subjected to vanity.

The race in which evil—that is, corruption, is at work, needs, as the one means of its rescue, subjection to vanity; it is the one hope against the supremacy of corruption; and the whole encircling, harboring, and helping creation must, for the sake of man, its head, and for its own further sake too, share in this subjection to vanity with its hope of deliverance.

Corruption brings in vanity, causes empty aching gaps in vitality. This aching is what most people regard as evil: it is the unpleasant cure of evil. It takes all shapes of suffering —of the body, of the mind, of the heart, of the spirit. It is altogether beneficent; without this ever invading vanity, what hope would there be for the rich and powerful, accustomed to and set upon their own way? What hope for the self-indulgent, the conceited, the greedy, the miserly? The more things men seek, the more varied the things they imagine they need, the more are they subject to vanity—all the forms of which may be summed in the word disappointment.

He who would not house with disappointment must seek the incorruptible, the true. He must break the bondage of havings and shows; of rumors, and praises, and pretenses, and selfish pleasures. He must come out of the false into the real; out of the darkness into the light; out of the bondage of corruption into the glorious liberty of the children of God. To bring men to break with corruption, the gulf of the inane yawns before them. Aghast in soul, they cry, "Vanity of vanities! all is vanity!" and beyond the abyss begin to espy the eternal world of truth.

The creation then is to share in the deliverance and liberty and glory of the children of God. Deliverance from corruption, liberty from bondage, must include escape from the very home and goal of corruption, namely death —and that in all its kinds and degrees.

If such then be the words of the apostle, does he, or does he not, I ask, hold the idea of the immortality of the animals? If you say all he means is, that the creatures alive at the coming of the Lord will be set free from the tyranny of corrupt man, I refer you to the poverty of such an interpretation. . . . Is God a mocker, who will not be mocked? Is there a past to God with which He has done? Is Time too much for Him? Is He God enough to care for those that happen to live at one present time, but not God enough to care for those that happen to live at another present time?

The new heaven and the new earth will at least be a heaven and an earth! What would the newest earth be to the old children without its animals? Barer than the heavens emptied of the constellations that are called by their names. Then, if the earth must have its animals, why not the old ones, already dear? The sons of God are not a new race of sons of God, but the old race glorified—why a new race of animals, and not the old ones glorified?

What lovelier feature in the newness of the new earth, than the old animals glorified with us, in their home with us—our common home, the house of our Father—each kind an unfailing pleasure to the other. Ah, what horses? Ah, what dogs! Ah, what wild beasts, and what birds in the air! The whole redeemed creation goes to make up St. Paul's heaven. He had learned of Him who would leave no one out; who made the excuse for His murderers that they did not know what they were doing.

The Coming Liberty

But what is this liberty of the children of God, for which the whole creation is waiting? The children themselves are waiting for it: when they have it, then will their house and retinue, the creation, whose fate hangs on that of the children, share it with them: what is this liberty?

All liberty must of course consist in the realization of the ideal harmony between the creative will and the created life; in the correspondence of the creature's active being to the creator's idea, which is his substantial soul. In other words, the creature's liberty is what his obedience to the law of his existence, the will of his maker, effects for him.

The instant a soul moves counter to the will of its prime cause, the universe is its prison; it dashes against the walls of it, and the sweetest of its uplifting and sustaining forces at once become its manacles and fetters. But St. Paul is not at the moment thinking either of the metaphysical notion of liberty, or of its religious realization; he has in his thought the birth of the soul's consciousness of freedom.

"And not only the creation, but we ourselves, who have the first fruits of the Spirit, groan inwardly as we wait for adoption as sons, the redemption of our bodies." We are not free, he implies, until our bodies are redeemed; then all the creation will be free with us. He regards the creation as part of our embodiment. The whole creation is waiting for the manifestation of the sons of God—that is, the redemption of their bodies, the idea of which extends to their whole material envelopment, with all the life that belongs to it. For this as for them, the bonds of corruption must fall away; it must enter into the same liberty with them, and be that for which it was created—a vital temple, perfected by the unbroken indwelling of its divinity.

The liberty here intended, it may be unnecessary to say, is not that essential liberty—freedom from sin, but the completing of the redemption of the spirit by the redemption of the body, the perfecting of the greater by its necessary complement of the less. Evil has been constantly at work, turning our house of the body into a prison; rendering it more opaque and heavy and insensible; casting about it bands and cerements, and filling it with aches and pains.

The freest soul, the purest of lovers, the man most incapable of anything mean, would not, for all his liberty, yet feel absolutely at large while chained to a dying body. The redemption of the body, therefore, the making of it for the man a geniune, perfected, responsive house-alive, is essential to the apostle's notion of a man's deliverance. The new man must have a new body with a new heaven and earth.

St. Paul never thinks of himself as released from body; he desires a perfect one, and of a nobler sort; he would inhabit a heaven-made house, and give up the earth-made one, suitable only to this lower stage of life, infected and unsafe from the first, and now much dilapidated in the service of the Master who could so easily give him a better.

He wants a spiritual body—a body that will not thwart but second the needs and aspirations of the spirit. He had in his mind, I presume, such a body as the Lord died with, changed by the interpenetrating of the creative indwelling will, to a heavenly body, the body with which He rose. A body like the Lord's is, I imagine, necessary to bring us into true and perfect contact with the creation, of which there must be multitudinous phases whereof we cannot now be even aware.

When the sons, then, are free, when their bodies are redeemed, they will lift up with them the lower creation into their liberty. St. Paul seems to believe that perfection in their kind awaits also the humbler inhabitants of our world, its advent to follow immediately on the manifestation of the sons of God: for our sakes and their own they have been made subject to vanity; for our sakes and their own they shall be restored and glorified, that is, raised higher with us.

Adoption as Sons

... The word *adoption* .... is used by St. Paul as meaning the same thing with the phrase, "the redemption of the body." In the beginning of the fourth chapter of his epistle to the Galatians, he makes perfectly clear what he intends by it. His unusual word means the father's recognition, when he comes of age, of the child's relation to him, by giving him his fitting place of dignity in the house; and here the deliverance of the body is the act of this recognition by the great Father, completing and crowning and declaring the freedom of the man, the perfecting of the last lingering remnant of his deliverance.

St. Paul's word, I repeat, has nothing to do with *adoption* [as we use the term commonly today]; it means the manifestation of the grown-up sons of God; the showing of those as sons, who have always been His children; the bringing of them out before the universe in such suitable attire and with such fit attendance, that to look at them is to see what they are, the sons of the house—such to whom their Elder Brother applied the words: "I said ye are gods."

If then the sons groan within themselves, looking to be lifted up, and the other inhabitants of the same world groan with them and cry, shall they not also be lifted up? Have they not also a faithful creator? He must be a selfish man indeed who does not desire that it should be so.